THE
FLYING
SUBMARINE

THE STORY OF THE INVENTION OF
THE REID FLYING SUBMARINE, RFS-1

Bruce D. Reid

HERITAGE BOOKS
2012

HERITAGE BOOKS

AN IMPRINT OF HERITAGE BOOKS, INC.

Books, CDs, and more—Worldwide

For our listing of thousands of titles see our website
at
www.HeritageBooks.com

Published 2012 by
HERITAGE BOOKS, INC.
Publishing Division
100 Railroad Ave. #104
Westminster, Maryland 21157

International Standard Book Numbers
Paperbound: 978-0-7884-3136-4
Clothbound: 978-0-7884-9194-8

*I dedicate this book
to the memory of my father,
who has been an inspiration, leader and
mentor throughout my life.*

*And I dedicate it also
to my beloved wife for her undying
patience, understanding,
sacrifice and support.*

Acknowledgements

I acknowledge and hold high praise for my friend Sharon Sarle, for her encouragement, wisdom and dedication to this project. She has spent countless hours providing structure and expertise to this, my first book.

Many thanks to my sister Carol and her husband Chuck Lazarr, who provided help and support throughout the evolution of the flying submarine.

I thank Russell A. Strine, President of the Mid Atlantic Air Museum for undertaking the task of retrieving, restoring and preserving the RFS-1 for all to see.

To the many friends and relatives who have inspired me to write this book, I say thanks.

Preface

The purpose of publishing this story is to recognize the inventor as an aviation pioneer and give readers a peek into the life of an interesting man and his unique invention.

This historical memoir has a time-line that spans from 1911 in Asbury Park, NJ, through the war on terrorism in Afghanistan and the 2003 war in Iraq.

It is a story of the trials and tribulations of inventor Donald V. Reid (deceased) as told by his son, the pilot of the world's first flying submarine (which can also be called a submersible aircraft). The book describes the flying sub, detailing the inventor's character, the inception of the flying submarine idea, its construction and testing, media coverage, documentary movies, and finally, the inventor's U.S. Supreme Court case and the ultimate disposition of the RFS-1.

Chapter 1. The Principals

AFTER A SUCCESSFUL AFTERNOON of water testing, he stood there in the tall grass in the middle of the airport taking 16-millimeter motion pictures of his newest creation as it accelerated down the runway for takeoff. As he watched with eager anticipation, something went very wrong. It left the ground and went out of control, suddenly rising straight up into the air like a rocket ship. His emotions jolted from elation to stark terror as he looked on with horror at the impending crash! These were the feelings of the inventor, Don Reid.

*   *   *

This story is about the RFS-1 Reid Flying Submarine (abbreviated to RFS-1). It could also be called a submersible aircraft. This is not a run-of-the-mill invention, and its creator was not an ordinary man. And it is the human story of the inventor and his life.

On May 18, 1911, Donald Vernon Reid made his first appearance on earth at 904 Bond Street, Asbury Park, NJ; he was born second of four brothers to Effie Layton Fields Reid and Burtt Augden Woodhull Reid. He was my father. And he invented, constructed, and tested the world's first flying submarine.

Don was different from most people, even somewhat

eccentric; he was a high-energy person of many interests and talents. He graduated from Bond Street Grammar School in 1927. He had already become a Boy Scout Tenderfoot of Troop 2 in 1924, and ascended the ranks of 2nd Class, 1st Class, Star and Life, culminating as an Eagle Scout in 1929. In January 1931, he became an assistant Scout Master.

Don attended Asbury Park High School on Sunset Avenue, where he honed his talent for music, playing such instruments as the piano, harmonica and accordion. His ambition and competitive spirit evidenced itself early, as he also became involved in sports: football, ice hockey and speed skating. His two upper front teeth were kicked out during an ice hockey game. Don was the Center in the New Jersey All-Star football team in 1927. He and his friend, Howard Roland (a local hero), also from Asbury Park, would frequently swim in the Atlantic Ocean from Asbury Park to Bradley Beach and back, a round trip distance of about two-and-a-half miles.

Don was instrumental in obtaining the first amateur radio station license, call sign W2AVN, for the New Jersey High School Radio Club. He received his high school diploma on June 17, 1932.

In spite of Don's varied interests, his technical aptitude stood out. He loved to solve problems for people, especially using unconventional means or work-around solutions, which might involve the use of new and unusual methods and techniques. Being an optimist, he had a positive outlook on nearly everything. People were amazed at his abilities when he demonstrated that the end results justified the means he used to accomplish an objective. "Tape, chewing gum and bailing wire" was not his mantra, but he surely excelled in their use. Like many scientific geniuses, he was not an extroverted, party-going socialite, although his congeniality permitted him to deal with the public easily. Prior to graduating from high school, he completed a technical course in the booming new field of radio at the RCA Institute at 75 Varich Street, New York City. That took a lot of effort because he had to thumb rides even in bad weather to get to those classes; he never missed one! He then opened his own radio repair store at 1237 Corlies Avenue in Neptune, NJ in 1931. Don placed a large loudspeaker on the roof of his model-T Ford truck and used it for advertising. On one notable occasion, he installed a public address system in Long Branch, NJ, for comedian Red Skelton's performances. He subsequently owned and operated a Harley Davidson motorcycle repair and dealership at the same address.

Don's later interest in the military was remarkable because he was not a militant man. He never owned a gun, did not hunt, and did not believe in killing for sport. He loved to fish, but even with rod in hand, his focus was on food instead of fun. When he caught a 45-pound striped bass off the 8th Avenue jetty in Asbury Park, he brought it home not as a trophy, but to feed his family. So mild-mannered was he that he did not use profanity or take the Lord's name in vain until much later in life. The very worst his family heard was "gol darn it!"; he was brought up that way, and he brought up his own family the same.

Don joined the National Guard of the United States and State of New Jersey at Headquarters Company, 2nd Battalion, 114th Infantry Division on July 11, 1929, at age eighteen. He continued through five consecutive enlistments. His fifth and final enlistment was in the 119th Observation Squadron, 44th Division Aviation of the NJNG. During his eleven-year military career, he earned medals as sharpshooter, marksman, expert rifleman and radio engineer. Much of his marksmanship was demonstrated at the Sea Girt Rifle Range. Don received his Honorable Discharge on September 6, 1940.

Don's humanitarian nature was evidenced in his active participation in volunteer efforts of the American Red Cross, a contribution that continued into his middle 70s. Throughout the 1940s, Don was very active in para-military organizations like the Civil Air Patrol, attaining the rank of Captain. In the late 40s and early 50s, he became a leader in the Civil Defense efforts of Monmouth County and established a Junior Cadet training group in radio communication, headquartered at his home in Wanamassa.

Don's marriage to June Nadine Sherman on January 27, 1933, in the Oakhurst Methodist Church produced three children: Dorothy Joyce, Bruce Donald, and Carol June. (I, Bruce Donald Reid, born September 10th, 1937, at Fitkin Hospital in Neptune, NJ, am the second principal in this memoir.) Dad was a faithful husband and father, as well as a good provider, even in the hard times. When he could, he traveled the country with his family on vacation. Being a reverent and honorable man, he regularly attended church while raising his family at the Trinity Episcopal Church at the corner of Asbury and Grand Avenues in Asbury Park.

Don respected authority and tried to live by the rules; he would not, in fact, even throw a candy wrapper from a car window because he knew that "someone else had to pick it up." He abstained from alcohol and tobacco. He believed in, and applied, strict discipline as a father, but never had to preach morality to his family because he set an example instead. Don was a kind, loving and considerate man. He would always take time to feed the squirrels and birds as they surrounded him and became part of his day. Though he had a heavy temper, it took a lot to provoke him. When something did rile him, you did not want to be around, because it was scary when he became very loud, with big bulging brown eyes. But that rarely happened.

Remarkably, he managed never to become vain or "holier-than-thou." Dad rarely talked to us kids about sports or the stuff of life like politics, or what was happening around the neighborhood, or how school was, or current events, or any mundane things. He never mentioned the "birds and bees" to me. I guess he knew that I would figure that out by myself when the time came for me to know. But as a family unit, we still maintained a firm bond and Christian values. Before we ever got that first ten-inch Sears Teletone television in 1947, we listened to all of the popular evening radio shows and played Canasta, Parcheesi or Monopoly. I cannot remember a time when my father took my mother out to a dance or social event, but he would occasionally take her or the family for a pizza or to a movie in Asbury.

My father was only five-foot-nine and weighed about 185-pounds. What he lacked in height, he made up for in character. Throughout his teens and twenties, he slicked his jet-black hair straight back. Then while in his 30s through 50s, he would slick it back only if he was going to work or going out for the evening; otherwise he wore it unkempt. The plaid shirt, work pants and a baseball cap became his identity while he worked in his yard, garage or basement workshop. During his retirement years, his hair turned to salt and pepper, and he sported a crew cut.

He was a stay-at-home person for the most part and usually worked in his cellar shop in the evening till 11:00 PM, while my mother watched TV. Many times she begged him to come up to bed and get some sleep. Don was a stubborn man, true to his astrological sign . . . Taurus. He would listen to people, perhaps even agreeing with them, but then do as he pleased.

Dad could be difficult at times. My mother pleaded with me sometimes to talk to him because he "always listened" to me. Well, that was not always true, but I could influence him. My mother had her moments with him, such as when she could not find her Kenmore canister vacuum cleaner one day. She asked him about it, and he said nonchalantly, "Oh, I was flying it this morning." He then went on to explain how he needed it for the motor of his new captive helicopter project! My father later told me that she was "a little upset" with him.

In another instance, in 1971, he was required to add air scoops for proper ventilation of his race boat, in order to pass a pre-race inspection for his entry in the Hennessy Grand Prix Offshore Power Boat Race in Point Pleasant, NJ. There was nothing lying around in the pit area of the Kings Grant Inn that he could use. And time was running out. So he got into his car and went all the way home to get the "parts," returning in record time to install them on the boat and pass inspection. He won the race in his class and received two trophies and $600. The next day, my mother reprimanded him rather severely after she discovered that a skeleton frame was all that was left of her once-shiny chrome-plated toaster! The sides of the toaster had made aesthetically pleasing and effective air induction scoops. He bought her a new toaster with the money. In this case, the end justified the means. The name of his boat was "Flying Submarine."

Don was a "show-and-tell" type, and that, too, annoyed his wife at times. For example, Don would often stop whatever he was doing with my mother and go out of his way to retrieve books, photos or anything relating to a project that he was working on, and explain in detail to anyone that showed interest in what he was doing. She would quietly look to the sky with that here-we-go-again look, and silently walk away. He often would go well beyond his listeners' curiosity.

When his wife asked him to do something in a specific way that he disagreed with, he would placate her by saying "Yes dear, yes dear," then turn around and do what he wanted to anyway.

Dad didn't start offshore powerboat racing until he was 60 years old! He bought his first boat from me for one dollar. It was a 21-foot boat that had been burned to the waterline, which I bought just for the engine to use on my own boat. He rebuilt it for a race, and continued to race and rebuild bigger broken boats for five years. He raced in the Hennessy for four years at Point Pleasant, Atlantic City, and the Benihana. (We both knew and liked Rocky H. Aoki, founder of the Benihana Restaurant chain. He was a neat guy who didn't have his nose in the air, and could (and did) blend right in with the crowd.)

Another phenomenal achievement in Don's busy and adventurous life was his participation in the World Championship Demolition Derby held at Langhorn Speedway in Pennsylvania in 1964 (sponsored by Spectacular Promotions of Islip, Long Island, NY). Although final victory eluded him, he made a good account of himself while driving a 1936 Buick Century, which later appeared on the TV show Wide World of Sports.

Being raised in a large, competitive family, and having survived our nation's great depression, Dad knew the value of things and believed in the old adage "one man's trash is another man's treasure." If he found something at the curb that looked good or had a shiny spot on it, he would say, "it's brand new." He would much rather repair a broken item than buy a new one, even if he could well afford it.

Dad was ahead of his time with another of his favorite sayings. Anytime someone was about to enter a car that my father was driving when he was in a hurry, he would say those now immortal words, "Let's roll!"

Throughout the years of raising his family in a rural setting, surrounded by woods, and later on after a housing development took over the area, Dad had some exotic pets that were out of the ordinary. In addition to dogs and cats, he had chickens that he raised for eggs, and which got loose periodically in his victory garden. He also had a de-scented skunk, but only for a short while, because being a nocturnal animal, it kept us awake at night by thumping loudly on the hardwood floors as it roamed the house. Later he had a pair of Peruvian Cavies (South American longhaired guineapigs). But the animal that got the most attention from people was the seven-foot Boa Constrictor. (It was only seven inches long when it was purchased in New York City.) He had that snake for about 18 years and kept it in a large, glassed-in tank in his living room.

*   *   *

Don worked for major defense contractors during the war years. He was an Aircraft Electrical Inspector at Eastern Aircraft Corp., Division of General Motors in Linden, NJ. To be closer to home, he took the job as Chief Electrician for navy aircraft crash, rescue and torpedo boats at Irwin Boat Works in Red Bank, NJ.

Working for the military eventually became the focus of Don's life. It was during a long and distinguished career with the Department of Defense that his creative genius flowered. There, he saw the needs and responded with solutions. While working for the Army and later the Navy as a civilian, he invented a host of items for military applications throughout the 1940s and 50s, ranging from large and complex to small and simple. For example, he designed and built a two-foot high model of a futuristic aircraft control tower, composed of four cylindrical main columns, with a tinted, glassed-in tower mounted atop. On the roof of this tower was mounted all required communications antennae, a white and blue rotating beacon, red obstruction lights and a weather station. One of the four vertical columns contained an elevator used to transport operations personnel to and from the tower. Contractors built the real operational control towers for the U.S. Government using this design.

Don became a design engineer for an operational, integrated control tower console. This was used inside of the real control tower to control the movement of aircraft both on the ground and in the air. It incorporated state-of-the-art communications equipment and a control panel with all of the necessary items to control many aircraft, including pockets or slots containing aircraft status cards for scheduled arrival and departure flight sequences.

My father invented a series of electric powered captive helicopters with counter-rotating rotor systems. ("Captive" means that the helicopter was tethered to one or more reels of wire, lines or cables, which provided electric energy to power, it, and a control used to operate any type of payload, such as a television camera, radar antennae, or remotely controlled gun.)

Don designed and constructed a mobile aircraft control tower at home, which could be picked up by helicopter from a trailer, flatbed truck or any other type of conveyance and swiftly moved to wherever air control was needed, without need of passable roads. This was shown in a demonstration with a twin-rotor Piasecki helicopter in a color motion picture at Monmouth County Airport (now called Allaire Airport).

He invented or helped to invent various types of antennae and communications systems. He invented special tools. Any one of these is a story in itself, and most are documented with papers, photographs and movies.

After his career with the military, he worked for a while as an Electronics Technician at the RCA Aerospace Center in Princeton, NJ. He worked on weather satellite, Gemini and Apollo programs.

When Don latched onto a project of his imagination, he became almost obsessed with it, and worked relentlessly to bring it to fruition. Very few projects were left unfinished. Although he only maintained below average to average grades in high school and never went on to college, one could say that his brilliance earned him the status of "engineer without portfolio."

Following the genetic intellectual profile of my father, I share many of his interests. I, too, had a long career in the Department of Defense. I have held my amateur radio license since 1966 and have a grasp of electro-mechanical fundamentals. I hold a U.S. Patent. And I was the pilot of the world's first flying submarine.

Chapter 2. The Inventor, Tinkerer

DON HAD A GOOD UNDERSTANDING of electro-mechanical principles. He had imagination, could improvise, and loved a challenge. And he liked doing things his own way.

The chain of events culminating in the RFS-1 story began when my parents were driving through New England and stopped in Groton, Connecticut, on January 24, 1954, to witness the launching of the world's first nuclear powered submarine, the NAUTILUS, USS-571.

Later, while driving home, he thought, "What a novel idea!" The concept of a radio controlled model submarine began to form. He reasoned that if there are radio-controlled model airplanes, cars and boats, why not submarines?

When he talked about his new idea to friends and co-workers, the skeptics said a radio could not work under water. That was the challenge which triggered his drive to prove them wrong! He had problems, of course. The first ballast tanks were . . . (are you ready for this?) . . . CONDOMS! In the 50s, one did not take them out of the bedroom, let alone show them in public, especially for a purpose for which they were not intended.

Don fiddled around and tinkered (what we call brain-storming these days) until he got his model to work. Though very primitive, my 1954 Christmas present was his first radio controlled (R/C) model submarine (Figures 2-1 and 2-2). I was very proud to own such a treasure and still have it today. The sub was three feet long, weighed 18 pounds, and could do all of the maneuvers a real sub could do: dive, surface, and turn. Don applied for his first U.S. Patent on July 8th, 1955 (Figure 2-3). On September 15th, 1959, after money, time and formality, a Patent was granted on a Radio controlled (R/C) Model Submarine: U.S. Patent No. 2,903,822.

Dad and I usually joined a group of between 10 and 20 fellow hobbyists and either flew R/C model airplanes in a large open field out near Colts Neck, NJ, or ran our R/C model boats at Sunset Lake in Asbury Park. We did this for many years on Sundays, if the weather was nice during the summer. The R/C model sub worked so well during demonstrations in front of spectators at Sunset Lake in Asbury Park, and in Lake Parsippany, that Don decided that he could actually manufacture them to sell to the world (Figures 2-4 through 2-7). The result was a side business manufacturing the subs for the hobby industry.

To do this, Don was advised to incorporate as a company. Money was tight, so he reasoned that it was cheaper to do it under his brother Burtt's housing construction company. He talked Burtt into allowing the creation of Reid Electronics, Division of Unit Production Corp. He then sold stock in the company to friends and co-workers for seed money.

Don made everything himself in the basement of his home, including drawings, gears, plugs, molds, and even big, powerful injection and vacuum molding machines for the hundreds of parts required (Figures 2-8 through 2-10). He made the radio equipment himself, so that the model subs could be sold either complete with everything, or without radios to those who preferred to use their own.

Dad also manufactured the drive train, brackets, props, shafts, couplings, gears, pumps, valves, rudders, dive planes, and hull parts. For the items that he could not make himself, he researched the model industry for off-the-shelf items such as electric propulsion and steering servo motors, wet and dry batteries, and special hardware. He did all of the milling, drilling, molding, finishing and painting. Don laid out all of the internal equipment and placed it all on or within a specially cut, flat plastic tray to contain and mount all of the accessories (Figures 2-11 and 2-12). He then would place the entire tray within a 3-inch diameter, 14-

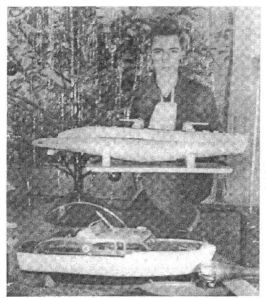

(Fig. 2-1) Bruce Reid holds the first operational R/C model submarine at Christmas, 1954.

(Fig. 2-2) The first operational R/C model submarine at the lake in 1954.

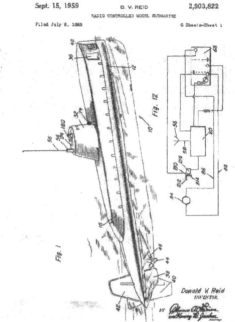

Sept. 15, 1959   D. V. REID   2,903,822

RADIO CONTROLLED MODEL SUBMARINE

Filed July 8, 1955   6 Sheets-Sheet 1

Fig. 12

Fig. 1

Donald V. Reid
INVENTOR

(Fig. 2-3) Figures 1 & 12 of Don's R/C model submarine patent.

(Fig. 2-4) Father and son show "Nautilus" at Sunset Lake in Asbury Park, NJ.

(Fig. 2-5) Don simulates giving orders to "Dive! Dive!" He uses the microphone with a switch to the transmitter during a demonstration at the Asbury Park Convention Hall, Inventor's Show.

(Fig. 2-6) Early sub running at "decks awash."

(Fig. 2-7) R/C sub running just below the surface.

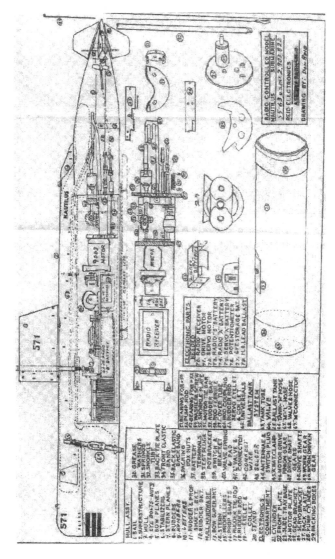

(Fig. 2-8) R/C sub parts drawing.

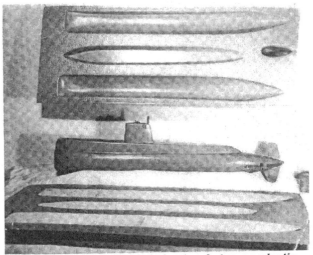

(Fig. 2-9) Vacuum formed sheets of styrene plastic. The sheet in the foreground contains three hardwood maple "plug" molds.

(Fig. 2-10) Homemade vacuum forming machines with a mold atop a stack of new plastic sheets.

(Fig. 2-11) An early model electronics compartment.

(Fig. 2-12) An electronics compartment with cylinder.

(Fig. 2-13) "Sailors" are standing on the removable clear plastic strip for running the sub on the surface.

(Fig. 2-14) Don holds a sub in his workshop. Notice the lead keel weight by his left hand.

ATOMIC ATTACK AIRPLANE, BOAT, or SUBMARINE

HAVE YOUR "R.C." OR "U" CONTROL MODEL

FIRE ATOMIC MISSILES

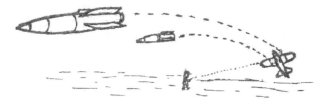

UNIVERSAL LAUNCHING BASE
ADAPTED FOR STANDARD ROCKETS

U. S. PAT.
2,003,022
OTHERS PENDING

FLYING TORPEDOES (FOR TEMPORARY OR PERMANENT MOUNTING BASES) TRAVEL FROM 300' TO ¼ MILE

REID ELECTRONICS

(Fig. 2-15) One of the many types of flyers Don made for his R/C sub business. Several different colored papers were used for labels and flyers.

(Fig. 2-16) Submarine line-up awaits paint. Other hull parts await cutting from formed sheets.

(Fig. 2-17) Don holds a Seawolf sub near the Nautilus production line.

inch long clear plastic cylinder called the electronics compartment, whose quarter-inch thick end plates were held in place and made waterproof with 2-inch wide elastic bands.

The completed cylinder was then placed within the two-piece, 37-inch long, plastic submarine hull, while simultaneously engaging the rudder coupling. After coupling the two propeller shafts to the shaft packing glands protruding from the rear end plate of the cylinder with quick disconnects, he hooked up the properly molded rubber ballast tank with a hose to the pump check valve, also on the rear plate. It sounds complicated, but it took less than half-a-minute to accomplish.

The inner workings were capped over with a top deck or superstructure, held in place with two tiny nuts, one in the front and one in the back (Figures 2-13 and 2-14). On the top of this top deck was a permanently affixed conning tower or sail, inside of which was a feed-through tube which allowed passage of the half-inch diameter, 18-inch long clear plastic snorkel tube used for air induction. This was screwed into the top of the electronics compartment cylinder within the sub. Since the conning tower was a sealed, air-tight unit, its buoyancy provided vertical stability to the sub.

A rigid steel wire radio antenna was fed through the snorkel tube, which was also used to activate a triple-pole switch. This switch provided power to three separate circuits: the propulsion motor which moved the sub through the water, the servo motor which turned the rudders and operated the ballast control valve, and the radio receiver which executed all of the commands.

Don did all of his own printing for large shipping labels, flyers, and operating instructions (Figure 2-15). This was done on a hand-cranked mimeograph machine typical of the 50s, before Xerox or modern copy machines were available for home use. He would search for used or discarded heavy cardboard cartons, then cut, fold and staple them for shipping boxes for the model subs.

Everything was done in an orderly manner: there were production lines for each part in a logical progression of need for assembly. Four family members helped out at night for a while, working the molding machines, cutting parts, packing and labeling shipping boxes (Figures 2-16 and 2-17).

Don bought out a small company in Neptune which produced

radio transmitters and receivers for the hobby industry (Figure 2-18). It came complete with all of the unfinished aluminum chassis and black crackle-finished housing cases, meters, vacuum tubes and sockets, wire, screws, and other vital components. Now Don would also hand wire, solder, finish and test all of the radio equipment. One must keep in mind that he still worked a full time job at the Naval Air Turbine Test Station in West Trenton, NJ, with a two-hour daily round-trip commute from his Wanamassa, home.

Don placed a tiny ad in the American Modeler magazine to sell these R/C subs. The response was mind-boggling. It became hard to keep up production to meet the demand. Over the next couple of years, he sold these R/C subs to nearly every state in the Union and to 17 foreign countries. The U.S. Government bought a complete R/C sub, as did the David Taylor Model Basin in Maryland. He made a large variety of subs (Figure 2-19).

The inventor continued experimenting with the size and complexity of these model submarines as well as expanding their capabilities. He developed a less complex, smaller and simpler Skipjack class model sub. Then he created several larger 5-foot R/C subs, modeled after the Sea Wolf, George Washington and Patrick Henry class subs (Figure 2-20).

Don continued to invent in the midst of all this activity, and on December 3, 1957, he applied for a patent on a Radio Controlled Torpedo. This model was about 18 inches long, had no ballast system or pumps, and could run about as fast as you can walk, using flashlight batteries for power. It had twin counter-rotating props on a single co-axial shaft. Two of these torpedoes could be housed within, and fired from, the hull of any of the larger R/C subs. He was granted his second Letters Patent on a Radio Controlled Torpedo on August 16, 1960, U.S. Patent No. 2,949,089 (Figures 2-21, 2-22 and 2-23).

My father was on a roll now. Although under-water rocket launching was not his idea, he developed a system for an under-water-to-air, chemically fueled rocket, which was fired from the under-water sub by radio pulse. This was done two years before the United States launched the first Polaris ICBM! The pinnacle of his genius in the field of R/C model subs was enabling the 5-foot George Washington sub to fire two R/C torpedoes, as well as

A RADIO TRANSMITTER
FOR THE HOBBY OF YOUR CHOICE

TRANSMITTERS FOR MODEL BOATS,
AIRPLANES, SUBMARINES, TORPEDOES.

REID ELECTRONICS
RADIO CONTROL HEADQUARTERS

(Fig. 2-18) Don's flyer for radio control equipment
that he manufactured and sold.

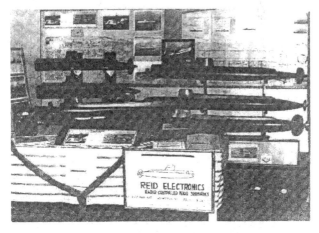

(Fig. 2-19) Production variety of R/C subs from a
28-inch Skipjack to the 5-foot George Washington.

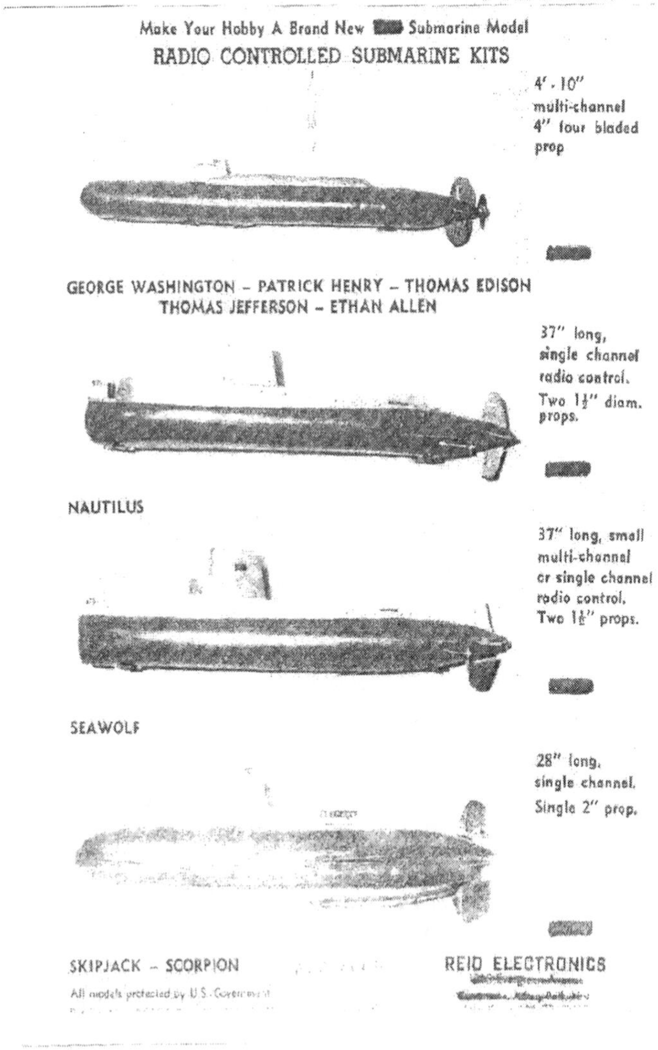

Make Your Hobby A Brand New ▓▓▓ Submarine Model

RADIO CONTROLLED SUBMARINE KITS

4' - 10"
multi-channel
4" four bladed
prop

**GEORGE WASHINGTON – PATRICK HENRY – THOMAS EDISON
THOMAS JEFFERSON – ETHAN ALLEN**

37" long,
single channel
radio control.
Two 1½" diam.
props.

NAUTILUS

37" long, small
multi-channel
or single channel
radio control.
Two 1½" props.

SEAWOLF

28" long,
single channel.
Single 2" prop.

SKIPJACK – SCORPION

REID ELECTRONICS

All models protected by U.S. Government

(Fig. 2-20) R/C sub variety with some specifications.

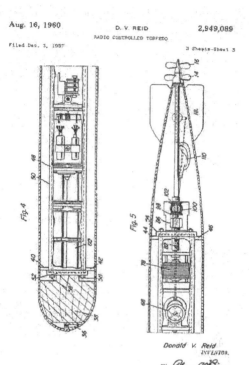

Aug. 16, 1960   D. V. REID   2,949,089

RADIO CONTROLLED TORPEDO

Filed Dec. 3, 1957   3 Sheets-Sheet 3

Donald V. Reid
INVENTOR.

(Fig. 2-21) Figures 4 & 5 of Don's R/C Torpedo Patent.

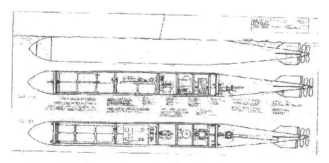

(Fig. 2-22) Torpedo parts identification drawing.

Submerged R/C sub fires a torpedo.

R/C torpedo under way.

(Fig. 2-23)

(Fig. 2-24) A cut-a-way view of a George Washington
sub with two R/C torpedos and rocket folded down.

launch the under-water-to-air rocket, all from a single channel radio. This was an astounding achievement, given the relatively primitive state of the art of radio control in the mid-1950s (Figure 2-24).

*   *   *

Alas, Don was an inventor, not a businessman. During the first half of the twentieth century, owning one's own business, usually a small shop or a retail store, was generally achievable by one person. But due to the complexity of Don's manufacturing business, exacerbated by the changing Post-World War II philosophy of business competition, specialization was required. My father would not accept the fact that he could not do it all by himself. With each facet of business being a specialized field (i.e. manufacturing, production, supply, advertising, and distribution), he was unwilling to "give away" his idea so that others could get rich.

Don tried to negotiate terms with several manufacturers interested in his work, but rejected the low percentage of profit they offered him. He would not accept of the idea that he could still get rich on low per-unit profit with high volume sales that large companies could produce. As a result, material costs rose and profits dwindled to zero like the domino effect. He finally paid off his stockholders and eventually went out of business and moved on to other things. What is it they say? Better to have tried and failed, than to never have tried at all. All in all, it was an exciting chapter in Don's life.

Chapter 3. And Then It Happened

THE RADIO CONTROLLED MODEL AIRPLANE is one of many hobbies that my father and I shared. Some of the model airplanes that we built had wingspans of more than five feet. These larger models had wings held in place with rubber bands so that they were easily detached for transport and storage, and so that they were less likely to incur damage from crash landings. Some of these were stored in my father's cellar workshop, usually up high and out of the way.

While Don was working in his cellar shop one night in 1956, a set of these model airplane wings accidentally fell from a shelf and landed across the hull of one of his R/C subs. He looked at it for a moment and thought, "WHY NOT? . . . WHY NOT A FLYING SUBMARINE?" That was the birth of an idea that would consume his every spare moment until he died!

Building a flying submarine requires a delicately balanced combination of aerodynamics and hydrodynamics. Don started out working with various model airplane parts and gas engines like the OK Cub .049 and McCoy .049 diesels mounted on top of the conning tower of one of his model submarines. Together, we started testing them at the softball field on Park Boulevard in Wanamassa, NJ, as a free flight model plane (Figures 3-1, 3-2 and 3-3).

We tried various wing, tail, and landing gear configurations. It worked pretty well, so he advanced the propulsion system to pulse jet engines because (a) he had them, and (b) he wanted to see what a sleek, fast one would look like and how it would perform. I designed and built the wings. They were made with a thirty-five degree sweep back, and planked with sheet balsa wood. Near the wing roots, the wings could be pivoted ninety degrees vertically, and folded back along the sides of the sub hull for under-water operation. This jet sub was powered by a Dyna-Jet, pulse jet engine which has propelled other models to nearly 180 miles per hour. They are flown at the end of two parallel ninety-foot stranded steel cable control lines. The Dyna-Jet was used on RFS-1 Mod 10 (Figures 3-4 and 3-5).

Designed after the German V-1 Buzz Bomb, the engine weighed one pound and could produce four and one quarter pounds of static thrust. It had the highest thrust-to-weight ratio of any jet of the period. Water didn't hurt the engine because it was essentially a hollow tube made of Monel, with reed valves and a fuel spray manifold mounted in a machined, red anodized aluminum head in the front. When a blast of air was used to start it, any remaining water would be blasted out of the back. We did not test it in free flight because of the certainty of local woods fires. If held and not permitted to fly after starting, it would turn white hot in less than a minute. I still have this sub.

We had two of these pulse jet engines. One was the Dyna-Jet, which used electric spark ignition to start it; the other was an M.E.W. 307 (Minnesota Engine Works), which used flame ignition at the back end. The latter was three inches in diameter and 26 inches long. Testing them in our neighborhood was interesting because of the extremely loud noise they produced. The instant it started, the sound caused my mother and sister Carol to jump off of the couch. There was not a squirrel or fowl within blocks after that loud, continuous 'bbaaaaaah' rattled the windowpanes all the way down the street. That engine was so loud that while holding it, you would not hear a person screaming at you from only a few feet away. We were lucky that the "law" did not pay us a visit. The engine was either off, or it started with the jerk of full power on, with no in-between.

Don designed, built and tested 13 actual working hobby

(Fig. 3-1) Bruce Reid with flying sub # 3 at the
Wanamassa ball field.

(Fig. 3-2) In flight at top, and just before landing at bottom.

(Fig. 3-3) FS #6 flares out for a perfect landing.

(Fig. 3-4) Inventor Don holds a jet powered flying submarine model 10 in his basement workship.

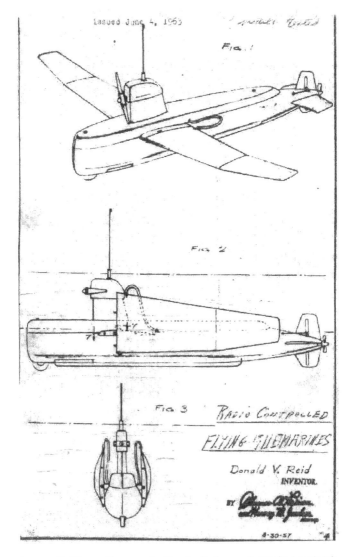

(Fig. 3-6) Three figures in Don's flying submarine patent.

models of this flying submarine to perfect its operation, flying each as a plane, then operating it as a submarine in Sunset Lake in Asbury Park. He applied for a patent on January 17, 1958, and was granted his third U.S. Patent on a Flying Submarine on June 4, 1963, Patent Number 3,092,060 (Figure 3-6). This patent covered any type of propulsion system (i.e. piston, electric and jet engines). It was later amended to include nuclear power. Further, the folding wing concept, folding propeller, and other configurations were also included in the patent.

The patent clearly states that variations in design, construction, and materials may be permitted to those skilled in the art. And that it is not desired to limit the invention to the exact construction and operation shown and described, and accordingly, all suitable modifications and equivalents may be construed as falling within the scope of the invention as claimed.

A strange coincidence is that we became aware after the fact that Donald Reid's home was located only a few blocks from where the Wright Brothers furnished five of their original airplanes for a ten-day air show in 1910. In the same town and vicinity of this site, Dad and I tested our very first models of flying submarines. The officials of the Township of Ocean, in Monmouth County, New Jersey, installed a memorial plaque on that site to commemorate the Wright Brothers historical event.

Chapter 4. The Real Thing

SATISFIED WITH MODEL PERFORMANCE, Don set out to build the real thing: a full size, man- operated flying submarine. The very thought of building something so challenging and bizarre, something that nobody had ever done before, elevated his determination to succeed. It is hard to imagine the amount of brainstorming and effort that this one man put into this project. Don was tenacious. He recalled the fictional sagas of the "Tom Swift" books by Victor Appleton, who was on the trail of flying submarines with two startling achievements, his <u>Submarine Boat</u> (1910), and <u>Flying Boat</u> (1923). Don did some research and found that there was nothing new in the idea of a flying submarine; even Leonardo Da Vinci mentioned a similar concept in his writings. As a matter of fact, there are U.S. Patents on similar devices dating back to the early 1800s and 1900s. What WAS new and different was that Don Reid not only talked about it, wrote about it, and patented it, but actually built one that was operational!

Dad had a vision of what his flying sub should look like, so he drove around the country from Maine to Florida, using his vacation time for about two years to obtain parts from nine different crashed airplanes. He traveled to small airports, some in rural areas, to find parts that he could use and afford, finding them mostly in crash pits or bone yards behind aircraft hangars.

For $100.00, Don located a 65-horse-power, Lycoming four-cylinder aircraft engine taken from a plane that had been demolished by a windstorm at Morrisville, Pennsylvania. Next was a used Sensenich wooden propeller, a pitot tube assembly from a navy "K ship" blimp, a Pioneer airspeed indicator, a complete Scott disengagable tail wheel assembly, and a pair of damaged Ercoupe wings with landing gear. These wings were from two different aircraft in two different locations. Tires and wheels came from several airports, including Palm Beach County Airport, Florida. In a salvage yard, Don found and bought five 80-gallon, aluminum, baffled fuel tanks that had been used in navy blimps. He also found some Link Trainer wings, an old roll-a-way bed frame made of steel angle iron with holes every inch or so, some flexible fiberglass sheet material, bolts, nuts, screws and sheet aluminum found in his basement workshop, and yes, a couple of galvanized garbage can lids. This is the stuff of the world's first flying submarine!

Subsequent full-scale flying subs were named with increasing numbers for each major structural change or rebuild, starting with "Mod" (model) 14. Minor changes to any model were denoted by a letter suffix. For example, RFS-1, Mod 23H was the twenty-third flying sub with eight minor changes to its design. Construction techniques were mostly trial and error. There was no "wind tunnel" testing. He continued to use materials that he could either scrounge or buy cheaply, as he had very little extra money.

*   *   *

Mod 14 was the first full-scale mock-up, loosely assembled in the side yard of his Wanamassa home on December 30, 1957 (Figure 4-1), with the help of his daughter Carol. This was a prototype, used for conceptual, photographic, and design feasibility studies only. Some of the original drawings were made from this model during the summer of 1958. But most of the drawings, sketches and diagrams were drawn "on the fly," meaning as they were needed. Many subassembly drawings were done as work-around solutions to solve problems encountered during the actual construction. Not all parts and assemblies had drawings. Also, there were construction departures from the

(Fig. 4-1) Carol Reid holds the propeller of RFS-1 Mod 14, the first full-scale mock-up in the side yard of Don's home.

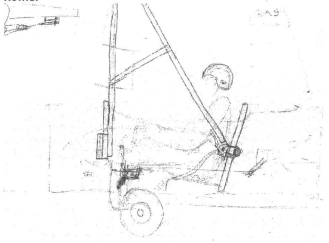

(Fig. 4-2) Rough drawing of Mod 15 pilot seat, showing the relationship of pilot to engine support frame and main wing spar.

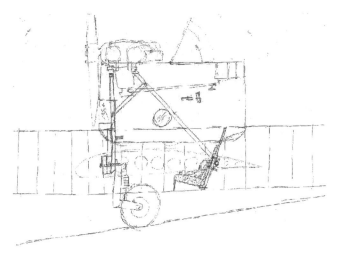

(Fig. 4-3) Rough drawing showing relationship of the conning tower frame, pilot seat and top exit door (not incorporated).

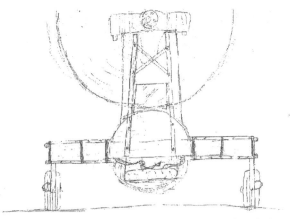

(Fig. 4-4) Rough drawing which shows a front view relationship of the main wing spar to hull, wing roots with landing gear, pilot seat with seatbelt, conning tower with engine on top of vertical mounting frame, prop arc and windshield.

original drawings, but they give some idea of the end results.

Since Carol was living at home with her parents, she was usually available. I, on the other hand, lived out of town with my own family, and had my own agenda. I would visit in the evening during the week on occasion, but I gave more time on weekends. Carol was an immense help to my father all through the RFS-1 development. She would assist by holding parts in place that Dad couldn't reach, and she would fetch, load, unload and carry materials, and much more. Later, her future husband, Chuck Lazarr would pitch in, too, when he was home on leave from the navy.

Mod 15 was a "fire-for-effect" model, to actually make the RFS-1 real, complete and operable. Don took the five 80-gallon tanks and lined them up end to end. He then joined them together by wrapping them with sheet aluminum shrouds between the tanks, and binding these shrouds with two-inch wide, spring steel shipping straps, pulled tight at the bottom with bolts. The RFS-1 was not built with longevity in mind, as salt corrosion would eat it up eventually. It was made to prove a point: that it could be done. And it could!

The cockpit was formed by cutting one end off of each of the second and third tanks from the front, then welding them together to form a capsule. The top area was cut out, and the internal tank baffles removed. This capsule would contain the pilot's seat, all controls, the instrument panel, and lower part of the engine. This also became the base for the conning tower. The main wing spar passed through the capsule at a location just in front of the pilot's knees (Figures 4-2 & 4-3).

The nose and tail cones were made by forming flexible fiberglass sheets into a conical shape, reinforced with garbage can lids placed at specific intervals as bulkheads. The thickness of the sheets made them stiff enough to act as a stressed skin without the need of stringers. The two edges of the sheets met at the bottom and were fastened to an aluminum keel strip running the length of each cone. The cones were then affixed to the appropriate end tank with steel band straps. The forward nosepiece (nose cap) was fabricated by laminating a number of wooden one-by-eights together, then cutting and milling them into a sort of prow, then mounting it to the front of the nose cone. On the back end of the tail cone was a three-inch opening where later a propeller shaft and bearing would pass. This completed the long, cylindrical hull.

The next crucial item was positioning and cutting of the two rectangular holes in the hull at the midship cockpit location, to allow passage of the wing main spar. The spar was actually made of two seven-foot long wooden two-by-sixes, spliced together side by side with bolts.

Don positioned the middle third of the main spar through the hull, leaving the outer thirds to protrude from each side of the hull. The two wing root sections were set into place on each side of the hull by inserting and securing the protruding wood main spars inside of each wing root, and mating them to the internal aluminum main spars of the wing roots. (The wing roots are short, stubby sections of the wing to which the landing gear is mounted, the inner edges of which were bolted to the hull.) The outer edge of each wing root is where the wing was pinned and bolted (Figure 4-4). This homemade main spar was so strong that it survived a crash, described later. The trailing (rear) edge of each wing root had an "L" shaped bracket placed against the hull and bolted at what we thought was the correct angle of incidence for this craft.

The outer main wing sections were mated to the wing roots by securing them with two heavy mounting pins on each wing, one at the top and one at the bottom, leaving about a two-inch space between the wing and root as originally designed. Two smaller bolts for each wing were placed into mating tabs near the rear edge to complete the job. A four-inch-wide aluminum strip covered the space between the wing and root.

Since the wings were designed for an Ercoupe with a tricycle landing gear configuration (meaning that it had a third wheel in the front) Don modified the wing, the landing gear mounting strut, and the cantilever angle, thereby changing the balance point in order to accommodate a conventional "tail dragger" (third wheel in the rear) landing gear. He used the Scott tail wheel by mounting it under the stern section (tail cone).

The following delineation of technical construction details and installation of other systems involved in the completion of the basic structure is significant both because there is nothing like it in the world, and also because it portrays Don's style.

The next structural group of items was the engine mount, conning tower and internal cockpit. This was the heart of the beast, tying everything together for strength. Now Don used that steel roll-a-way bed frame by cutting two main vertical front engine support members from it, then bolting them to the wooden wing main spar at the correct spacing inside the cockpit to mount the engine high enough overhead that the propeller arc would clear the top of the hull in front of what would become a conning tower. He then made two more, longer engine support members, which ran from the engine rear mounts at an angle downward toward the rear of the cockpit, and fastened to the upper sides of the hull. Criss-cross members and other stiffeners and brackets were placed where required for strength. At the top of the four steel members, Don placed brackets to support the four rubber engine mounts. The Lycoming engine was positioned on top of these mounts, and bolted into place, then safety wired.

With the engine and main mounting structure completed, Don proceeded with other reinforcements. The front of the tower was made of a single piece of one-eighth-inch thick aluminum, curved around to form a smooth leading edge of the tower, thereby minimizing wind resistance from the propeller slipstream just in front of it. This vertical, curved piece was attached to each side of the two vertical engine support members. Near the bottom of this curved piece was a square, curved window of Plexiglas. Just over that window was a hole that supported a piece of household rain downspout, used for air induction to supply air to the engine carburetor.

The back of the tower was made from a symmetrically curved piece of rain gutter, mounted at a slightly forward-swept angle to the back of the cockpit at its base. The top of the gutter was fastened to the back of a one-inch thick, bullet-shaped wooden shelf-like support structure, placed just behind the engine, which also became a base mount for a five-gallon, gravity feed motorcycle gas tank used to provide fuel for the aircraft engine.

Don added an outer metal skin to give it the shape of a submarine conning tower and streamline it (Figure 4-5). It was made from a sheet steel advertising sign for Lucky Strike cigarettes. The starboard side was made from one piece, curved around the side of the tower from the trailing edge rain gutter to the leading edge vertical aluminum window structure. The port side was made from two pieces, with a piano hinge joining the two near the middle, and placed at a forward swept angle to match the trailing edge of the tower. The top and bottom of the skins were fastened to the wood gas tank support shelf and side edges of the cockpit respectively, except for the door. This door was used to enter and exit the cockpit. At eye level of the sitting pilot were two windows cut in the shape of round portholes on each of the side skins; these were covered with Plexiglas.

The next item on the agenda was to wire up and instrument the engine. Don mounted the propeller to the engine after he cut off a part of the end of each of the two prop blades so that they would clear the top of the hull by a few inches. Then he wired the two engine magnetos to a "mag" switch, mounting it along with an aircraft plunger type priming system to an instrument panel in the conning tower, just below the windscreen. Next, he wired up a cylinder head temperature gauge and connected an oil pressure gauge.

I was able to provide expertise in various forms of instrumentation throughout the RFS-1 evolution, as that was my business while working for the Federal Government at that time. Don hooked up a tachometer which I constructed, pending the acquisition of a more correct one. My "tach" was made from a tiny tach-generator which provided seven volts per thousand rpm. After mounting it to a structural member, it was connected to the flexible tach cable (like a speedometer cable) to the back of the engine. The output voltage was fed to a voltmeter, with a custom dial face to represent rpm times ten. It was very accurate. These were the minimum gauges needed to monitor engine performance.

*   *   *

We were both anxious to see if it would run, even before we finished building it. It was time to play! Dad put cement blocks in front of the wheels to act as chocks so that the RFS-1 would not move forward, and then tied the back down to a tree trunk in his back yard.

With basic instrumentation installed, Don fueled up the gas tank, turned on the fuel valve, primed the engine, gave it some

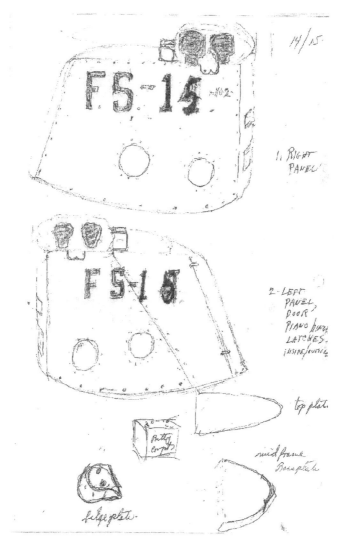

(Fig. 4-5) Rough drawing of conning tower exterior skin with portholes. Only one pair of ports was used.

(Fig. 4-6) "Link trainer" wings serve as tail assembly on Mod 15, and a small boat propeller is seen at the stern.

(Fig. 4-7) Don Reid proudly stands by Mod 16, showing new twin tail.

throttle; he then went around to the right side of the RFS-1, and with one hand, "propped" it a couple of times, turned on the mag switch to "both," and yelled "CLEAR!" With both hands on the prop, he threw his right leg forward, then back to gain momentum as he swung the prop hard. Nothing happened! After about ten more tries, fuel began to run all over inside the cockpit. The problem turned out to be only a gummed up carburetor that had been sitting around for years. He cleaned it (and the spilled gas) up and finally started the engine, which sounded great. It even idled down smoothly.

After checking the engine temperature and oil pressure, Dad looked at me, paused for a moment with "that" grin while standing outside the cockpit. You know the grin I mean? The one people use when they know that something devilish was about to happen. Then he reached in for the throttle and opened it as wide as it would go. The rpm went to 2650, and the sound of the four open exhaust stacks was deafening. The machine was shaking as if to say, "Let me go!" With all of this commotion going on, we did not see that the air blasting back from the propeller had blown all the white sheets off of our neighbor's clothesline, leaving them in the dirt. He shut the engine down with great excitement. Then there was silence as we turned to see the neighbor woman with arms folded, glowering at us at the property line. Let me tell you that all hell broke loose. If we thought that the Lycoming was loud, we got a big surprise! She eventually got over it . . . I think.

*   *   *

Without a working tail assembly, Don used the Link Trainer wings to simulate a conventional tail until he could locate something better (Figure 4-6). He temporarily mounted them to the fiberglass tail cone with the help of metal straps to hold them in place. He finished off Mod 15 with a paint scheme similar to that of real submarines of the era: black hull, wings and tail, with a gray superstructure and conning tower. Mod 15-F was the last of that series, completed in June of 1961.

Mod 16 came about after making major changes to the structure of the RFS-1. Don found a damaged twin tail of yet another Ercoupe and decided to use it (Figure 4-7). He repaired damage to the left rudder and cleaned it up. This tail section was mounted to the fiberglass tail cone with long bolts and wood wedges to hold it in position. This changed the center of gravity of the RFS-1.

The center of gravity was frequently checked and adjusted throughout the evolution of the RFS-1. To do this, Don would set up his "balance check system" by first jacking up the RFS-1 off the ground about a foot, then setting up two piles of timber and cement blocks with a round balance rod positioned on top of each block. This was all precisely positioned under each wing root at a place we call the center of lift. The RFS-1 was then lowered onto the balance rods. Weights were added either forward or aft to achieve balance.

Flight controls were designed, fabricated and installed. This was accomplished by placing a metal control stick with a plastic handgrip into a ball socket located in the middle of the cockpit, at the bottom, between the pilot's legs. The stick protruded out of the bottom of the cockpit (Figure 4-8). Control rods were connected to the bottom of the stick, using ball bearing clevises and support eyes; these rods ran the length of the hull bottom toward the tail. The outer ends of these rods were connected to the appropriate bellcranks of both the wings and elevator assemblies. A foot-powered rudder bar, similar to the steering bar on an old-fashioned snow sled provided rudder control. It was mounted to the cockpit floor so that the pilot's feet could turn the rudder. External stranded steel cables were connected between the rudder bar and rudders, using feed-through pulleys at the tail cone. There were two additional short cables connected to tension springs attached to the tail wheel so that when the rudder was turned, so too was the tail wheel.

The pilot sat in the cockpit in a low seat made of plastic webbing from a lawn chair, with the engine carburetor just over his head, and in front of him. The seat belt used was from the passenger side of my 1956 Ford Thunderbird (I still have this car). When the engine was running, it was very noisy inside.

It was during this period, when the RFS-1 was nearing completion, that I was conducting a few tests of the engine and other things and had an accident with the RFS-1. Would you believe that? The RFS-1 was untethered, except for two wheel

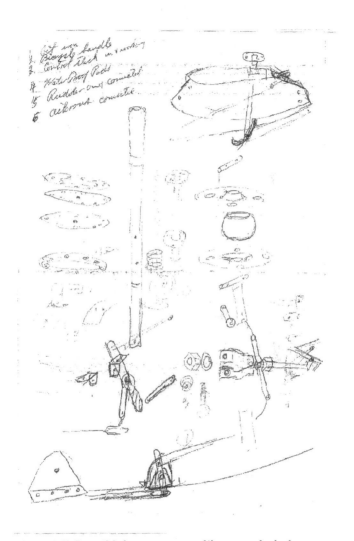

(Fig. 4-8) Don thinks on paper with an exploded view of the control stick assembly with ball and socket. Control rods were connected at the bottom end by clevises on the outside of the hull.

(Fig. 4-9) The hull shows a dent (left side of photo) after Mod 15 was jammed between the right rear of the Buick and trees.

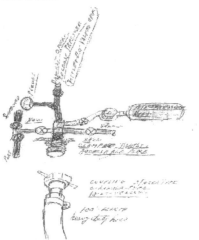

(Fig. 4-10) Drawing shows two theoretical air sources feeding an air manifold, a compressed air tank and an external air supply hose.

chocks, one of which was a piece of cement block, the other a short two-by-four. While running the engine alone one day, I applied full throttle to monitor the rpm and oil pressure. The RFS-1 pushed away the cement block piece and jumped over the two-by-four as it lurched forward across the side yard before I could stop the engine. With no brakes to stop it (they were never installed, to reduce weight), the RFS-1 headed for my uncle's 1936 Buick Century, which was parked in the yard by some large trees. As I looked out through the front window for the first time, over this long sword-like bow, my heart was pounding. I could see that I was about to collide with the trunk of the car! Using the never-before-tested rudder bar, I made the bow swing to the right, narrowly missing the back of the car, but wedging the flying sub nose between the right rear fender of the car and a tree before it stopped. Luckily, there was only superficial damage to the sides of the nose cone, which was easy to repair. As for the car; there was no dent, only scraped paint. They just don't build them that way any more (Figure 4-9).

*   *   *

Don had a propulsion system that would allow flight through the air, but now he needed a system to push the RFS-1 through the water. This is where he departed from convention. He wanted to keep the propulsion system simple, and in order to reduce weight for flight on Mod 16 and future variants made it removable. The system was built on a plywood platform, using a Chevrolet starter motor, solenoid and storage battery. He was not concerned about waterproofing it, because this motor would run even while under water. Again, he was not terribly concerned with how long it lasted or how efficient it was. (While these factors were clearly not the center of his focus, they were nonetheless necessary.) He made a direct drive to the prop shaft with no reduction or gearing. Switch wires were run from the solenoid to the cockpit to energize the motor. The whole thing was removable with quick disconnects.

The RFS-1 now had a body, wings, tail, conning tower with controls and two propulsion systems, but now he added one more item: a ballast system. This would enable the craft to submerge under the water, then resurface fully. Controlling the amount of air over the water within each tank was really simple. Each of the 80-gallon tanks had a four-inch diameter hole in the bottom, where fuel fittings used to be attached. These would be permanently open to the sea. Water would freely enter for submerging and exit when blowing ballast to surface.

Two air sources were made available within the cockpit; one air source was from an internal high-pressure storage tank of compressed air at three thousand psi through a reduction regulator (Figure 4-10). But repeated commercial refills could become costly with frequent use. The other air source was from an external low pressure air supply that was fed through a two-inch hose connected to two shore-based low pressure, high volume electric air compressors. (Figure 4-11) Since our initial water tests would be captive in nature, meaning not under way, and in a small lake at the airport, it was much cheaper and more practical to use the latter method than to make the RFS-1 self-sufficient.

On the left side of the cockpit, Don installed a main air induction manifold to facilitate the connection of either air source (Figures 4-12 and 4-13). He connected four large, specially modified valves to the manifold, controlled from inside the cockpit. These valves were four-way attitude control valves. (My wife would like to know where she could get some to install on me.) The main ballasting was accomplished using these valves arranged in a specific pattern for operation. For redundancy, there were two independent systems, a primary and a secondary, should one fail. Rubber garden hoses ran outside of the hull from the air valves to each ballast tank through a fitting connected to the top of each of the three remaining tanks of the hull, one forward, and two aft in series. This was known as the primary ballast system.

Also connected to the main manifold were secondary air-lines running from separate air valves and lines to the nose and tail cones. Should a hose get cut or blown off a fitting, the other independent system was thought to be sufficient to surface the sub. The combination of these four valves had the ability to put air into the ballast tanks to surface, and to exhaust the air back out of the tanks to submerge. Changing the pitch (angle on the bow) could be accomplished by putting more air in one end than the other. Additional air in the bow, for example, would leave the bow

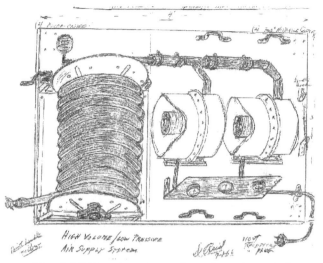

(Fig. 4-11) Drawing shows two shore-based air compressors with a 2-inch hose on a reel.

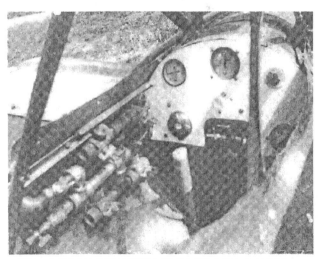

(Fig. 4-12) Instrumental panel with wing control valves at bottom center, and four main ballast air valves on left side.

(Fig. 4-13) Main air manifold with two air sources at left. The top two valves are primaries, two bottom valves are secondarys, two front valves are for the bow, and two back valves are for the stern.

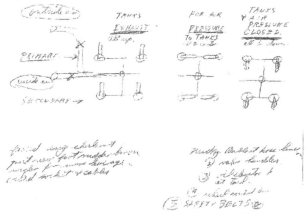

(Fig. 4-14) Drawing shows air sources from both internal and external at left, with primary and secondary valves. It also shows air distribution to ballast tanks.

higher than the stern.

These four valves were arranged in a simple, logical and specific pattern: the top two were used as the "primary" system, while the bottom two were used as the "secondary" system; of the four valves, the two facing forward controlled the bow, while the two facing aft, controlled the stern (Figure 4-14).

Additionally, there was another line extending from the main air manifold running forward to the bottom center of a new, white instrumentation panel. This air pressure line fed four smaller air control valves arranged in the pattern of a cross. The top control valve provided air into the other three. The right and left control valves fed air to the port and starboard wings, respectively, through hoses which ran out to air bladders in each wing tip. Each bladder had pressure relief valves in the bottom to relieve any excess pressure. The bottom control valve was used to vent (exhaust) air from the wings. These valves controlled the tilt, or side-to-side bank angle of the sub.

The instrumentation ensemble for under-water operations was provided in the form of a home-made dual axis bubble level, depth gauge, compass, air manifold pressure gauges, flash light, sound powered phones for communications, and crossed fingers for luck.

I used to sit in the cockpit and practice valving while imagining the response with closed eyes. There were no books or instructions on how to do this, so the RSF-1 became, in effect, my static flight and submarine simulator. I'm glad I did this, because it became near life saving later on.

So there it was. The operation was simple: air on top pushing water out of the bottom to surface the sub, and vise versa to submerge. The sub's pitch and depth were controlled by selecting a combination of those four valves on the left side to control ballasting for level, submerging and surfacing, or for bow up or down, or for just holding neutral buoyant position. It took less than two pounds per square inch of air pressure to hold the sub at full surface. Over pressure could not hurt anything, because the air would simply bubble out of the four-inch openings in the bottom of the tanks once the sub was fully surfaced. (When it did, it made a loud rumbling sound inside.)

How deep will it go? How fast? How high? How far? The following are some specifications and statistics. If the RFS-1 was just below the surface, it was submerged! The RFS-1 was not designed to break depth, speed, altitude or endurance records. It was designed to go about two knots while submerged, and four-and-a-half knots on the surface, using the electric motor. There were many variants of the RFS-1, weighing from 650 to 1400 pounds empty. It was 26 feet long, with a 28-foot, 4-inch wing span, and stood 7 feet, 2 inches high. It had a take-off speed of about 62 mph, a stall speed of about 56 mph. Cruise and top speeds were estimated to be 80 and 95 mph respectively.

.   Another logical question is frequently asked. How does one keep the aircraft engine dry while submerged? This was accomplished by first removing the propeller, then covering the entire conning tower with a rubberized World War II bomber gas tank, and lashing it down to the hull at the base of the conning tower. This reflects the Bell principle, like taking an empty water glass, turning it upside down, and then placing it under water. Air becomes trapped inside at the top. The cockpit partially fills with water as the RFS-1 submerges, with the pilot's upper body and engine staying dry within the trapped air of the upper conning tower. For safety, Scuba gear was stored aboard for emergencies.

Chapter 5. The First Tests

BY THE SUMMER OF 1961, the RFS-1 was complete with all systems. Now it was time to see if it all worked. The initial research and development phase had been accomplished, so it was time for the test and evaluation phase of Mod 16.

Don made a special hook-up to tow the RFS-1 to what was then the Asbury Park Air Terminal, located just south of Route 66 and just east of the Garden State Parkway in Neptune, New Jersey (Figure 5-1).

First, the wings were removed from the RFS-1, then placed one atop the other on the roof rack of his 1954 Plymouth station wagon, and tied down securely with nylon webbing. Next, a large plank was fastened down inside of the car so that one end of the plank stuck out a few feet beyond the tailgate. Then the tail wheel of the RFS-1 was lifted onto the end of this plank and tied down, allowing the RFS-1 to be towed backwards on its own main landing gear wheels like a trailer. This lash-up was somewhat precarious and prevented Dad from making any sharp turns, but it worked. The rest of the support equipment and tools were loaded into the back of the station wagon.

Off to the airport we both would go, towing Mod 16 at speeds of no more than 10 to 25 miles per hour, causing some frustrated, angered and amused drivers to gesture and verbalize when they could pass us. I remember sitting in the back of the wagon, making sure everything stayed put during transit, and seeing the faces and gestures of the other drivers and passengers. We had to start out early in the morning because of the immense, time-consuming effort required to get the RFS-1 to the airport in weekend traffic, then assemble, test, disassemble and bring it home, all in the same day and before darkness descended.

Don was a long-time acquaintance of U.S. Navy Commander Isaac Schlossback (Ret), who accompanied Admiral Richard E. Byrd on his second scientific expedition to Antarctica in 1933. Ike owned the airport. The RFS-1 was named in his honor and is mentioned in a Neptune Township publication entitled Ike's Travels by Peggy Goodrich.

Once at the airport, we prepared the RFS-1 by reassembling it to make it operational again. Curious on-lookers followed us in to see what we were up to with this strange-looking machine. Many were reluctant to ask questions, while others asked and were astonished with the answers Don provided. He delighted in talking about it.

The first tests listed in the flight syllabus were a series of taxi tests to check maneuverability. Speed would be increased in subsequent test runs. If it was controllable at high speeds, flight attempts would be made to fly just off of the ground, then back down again. That was the agreement Don had with Ike. The pilot recorded all remarks after each test run on a kneepad. Throughout the evolution of the RFS-1, I did most of the testing, but not all; my father can be seen in many of the historical photos.

We tested the RFS-1 only on weekends because we both worked during the week. But on weekends the airport activity was at its busiest. So finding a "window," or time slot, in an uncontrolled airport was a challenge. We had to be vigilant and very alert to use the runways between regular air traffic takeoffs and landings. We had to expedite our activities when the opportunity presented itself by getting onto the runway, doing our thing, then getting off and out of the way, even on the narrow taxi strips. This also required a lot of patience.

The airport itself had its own peculiarities, which were difficult to deal with at times. For example, the longest runway was listed on aeronautical sectional charts as 3,000 feet, but it was really only about 2300 feet. The main runway was an unpaved

(Fig. 5-1) Aerial view of State Route 66 and Asbury Air Terminal, grass landing field near the upper center.

(Fig. 5-2) An aircraft on final approach to land, close to the edge of Route 66. The Jumping Brook Golf & Country Club water tower can be seen at the upper left, between the wing struts.

(Fig. 5-3) The instant that the engine fires up.

(Fig. 5-4) Don Reid runs along side of Mod 16 with movie camera in hand as it taxied down the runway.

(Fig. 5-5) Inventor Donald V. Reid is seen inside the cockpit of Mod 16 on the rough, cross-wind runway after shutting it down and rolling to a stop.

mixture of hard dirt, gravel and grass, which ran at an incline from west to east, toward the Jumping Brook Golf and Country Club. This was runway 9. (Going west, naturally it would be runway 27.) There were no actual numbers on the runway thresholds, and it didn't matter to us anyway.

The crosswind runway was even shorter, starting from very near the edge of Route 66 at one end and ending with a tall stand of trees at the other end (Figure 5-2). It was nearly all grass which when wet, uncut or both presented even more of a challenge. We generally did high-speed tests on the uphill runway 9 to help in stopping when we went long near the end of the runway.

We put the RFS-1 through some of its paces for the first time and discovered some areas which needed to be corrected (Figures 5-3 through 5-5). This was anticipated. First of all, the pilot had extremely limited visibility and was in danger of running into the path of moving aircraft. Sitting well back in the cockpit, looking out of a relatively small window in the front, he literally had tunnel vision. This was very dangerous. The yaw (side to side steering motion of the nose) axis was very sluggish in response to rudder inputs, which created an over-steer condition. This was an inherent characteristic because of four factors; first, the twin rudders are small; second, only one rudder responds to an input at a time (not both); third, neither rudder was directly in the propeller slipstream; and finally, the length-to-weight ratio caused a dynamic moment arm. The wing angle of attack was too shallow to provide enough lift for flight, even at speed with the tail down.

Our intent was not to actually take off during this phase of testing, but rather "feel light," or do short, controlled hops off of the ground. By day's end, we found out a lot about the performance and returned home with a sense of pride and accomplishment, our heads full of new ideas to try out.

Don started work right away with these fresh ideas and changes to implement. He did this throughout the summer and fall of 1961, testing, changing, testing, changing. In most cases, the changes improved performance or corrected problems, but he needed money to buy more and better parts.

Don continued to make more changes to Mod 16 in 1962, and incorporated additional windows in the sides of the conning tower.

He reduced the length of the stern by about two feet to help correct the yaw problem, increased the wing angle of incidence, and added running lights. He also replaced the wooden nose cap with a symmetrical, bullet-shaped plastic one made from a large flowerpot. These and other minor changes were implemented just prior to the next series of tests, which were to take place before the winter set in.

Chapter 6. Sound the Klaxon. Dive! Dive!

ON A GLORIOUS FALL SATURDAY IN 1962, my father and I were prepared to try Mod 16 as a submarine for the first time. There was a small lake or pond at the airport, more than 100 feet in diameter and ten feet deep in some areas. In places it dropped off suddenly near the edge. This pond was there for Ike's two horses to drink from when they were allowed to roam the airport grounds freely. (There was never an incident or problem with the horses doing that, as far as I know.)

After the RFS-1 was assembled, I taxied it around for a while; then it was time to "go for broke." Don took some precautions for this first time because he did not know what might happen once we were committed to the water. He laid out about 100 feet of very heavy nylon webbing near the edge of the water, tying one end to the bumper of his 1961 Mercury Comet station wagon. This was in case he might need to pull it up out of the water with his car if the RFS-1 broke up, sank, or went out of control.

Don also prepared the land-based air supply by running a heavy electrical extension cord from a nearby building and connecting it to the switch of two high volume air blowers used as air compressors. A long, two-inch diameter hose ran from the blowers, across the pond, to the launch site at the east edge of the pond. This was done in case emergency air was needed in a hurry.

My father gave me the signal that all was ready. As I taxied up to the edge of the pond and stopped, he tied the other end of the nylon safety line to both landing gear mounts using a bridle arrangement while the engine was running.

While sitting in the cockpit in my scuba diving wet suit, I turned off all of the ballast control valves to hold the RFS-1 at full surface after it entered the water. Upon Dad's signal, I applied some power. The RFS-1 started to move forward as the wheels eased down the drop-off and into the water. With the bow in the water and the body of the hull stuck on land, I gave it more power while Dad helped by pushing. The RFS-1 moved forward into the water at full surface, and moved out across the pond very nicely (Figure 6-1). (A mix of both Mod 16 & 17 photos are used to describe events).

There were a few holes in the crotch area of my old wet suit, and I soon felt the cold water as it came rushing in through holes in the bottom of the cockpit (as designed). I was very nervous at this point, but settled down after a couple of minutes and made a sweeping turn to the right (Figures 6-2 and 6-3). Then I was stopped about three-quarters of the way around, by a shallow outcrop of land.

I shut the engine down as Dad waded out, got behind the left wing, and manhandled the craft back over near the car. I checked all of the gages, heard no leaking or bubbling, then exited the RFS-1 with an air of confidence (Figure 6-4). A group of curious on-lookers gathered around and watched our every move. Twelve ducks paddled over near us and did the same (Figures 6-5 and 6-6).

A side note: unlike the TV series, Voyage to the Bottom of the Sea, the RFS-1 was not designed to come down from the sky and crash into the ocean at speed, and continue on its mission. Neither machine nor human being could withstand the forces imposed by such a concept. It was only future missions of flying submarines in general which would land on the surface of the water like a seaplane, then submerge to accomplish its mission, resurface, and take to the air again like a seaplane. In Don's analogy, he stated "Like a newborn baby, it needs to crawl before it walks." The RFS-1, being in its infancy, needed to be prepared for flight. Future flying submarines would take on a seamless transition to land on the water, submerge, resurface and take off, or any

(Fig. 6-1) Powering Mod 16 into the water for the first time.

(Fig. 6-2) Powering Mod 16 around in a circle to the right.

(Fig. 6-3) Mod 17 is stopped at waters edge.

(Fig. 6-4) Bruce Reid exits the RFS-1 Mod 17 wearing a wet suit.

(Fig. 6-5) Even the ducks were curious.

(Fig. 6-6) The ducks look on as we prepare Mod 16 for the first dive.

(Fig. 6-7) Removing the propeller before covering the conning tower.

(Fig. 6-8) Don stands on a submerged out-crop of land as the RFS-1 is cautiously tested for the first time.

combination thereof, as the state of the art advanced. As back-yard mechanics, we were limited in capability and funding, as opposed to a large corporation funded by the government.

The RFS-1 now needed to be prepared to dive. Although a folding propeller concept was covered in the patent and is shown in those drawings, we did not have one, and therefore needed to remove the propeller so that the rubberized cover could be placed over the top of the conning tower (Figure 6-7).

As we prepared the RFS-1 for its first dive, on-lookers were showing amazement at what they had just seen, which opened a floodgate of questions. Dad kept right on working on it while he delighted in answering their questions and explaining what he was doing.

After the pitot tube and air instruments were sealed off from water intrusion, and other items checked off the list, I was ready to meet the challenge. I climbed into the cockpit and closed the door.

Now Don picked up the heavy rubberized cover and placed it over the top of the engine, pulling the bottom edges down near the hull. There were six eyebolts used to secure the bottom edge of this cover; these were tied down to the wing roots with rope.

Although I had a knife with me, I would not be able to open the door to cut those lines if something went wrong. I was not claustrophobic at that time, but with no escape possible, I did have some very anxious moments while under water.

Don pushed the RFS-1 backwards, over nearer to the compressors, and connected the external air line to the air manifold on the left side of the cockpit. He also handed me the sound-powered phones from under the bottom edge of the door; these were hung up high inside the cockpit so that they would not get wet. Wires to a phone set on land connected them. I checked my scuba back-up air system inside, while Don turned on the compressors.

These initial static tests were done without electric propulsion. So Don pushed the RFS-1 back out into deeper water and said "You're clear! Go ahead!" With that, I opened all four main valves to exhaust. For just a few minutes, I felt water coming in and air rushing out, as the RFS-1 settled in the water to about half submerged; then I nervously locked all valves closed again. I waited in silence to see what was happening.

As I successfully tried combinations of valve settings for bow up, bow down, and for various attitude changes, I allowed deeper dives. I also tried ballasting the wings for bank angle. The operational controls of the RFS-1 were actually quite good (Figures 6-8 through 6-13). Only a few changes were needed to correct some quirky things that happened during tests.

We tested the RFS-1's diving capabilities several times and encountered some interesting problems and terrifying experiences. For example, on the very first deep dive, meaning totally submerged, the water level came up much higher inside of the conning tower than it should have. The water came up to my nostrils, with my head jammed up against the engine carburetor near the top of the conning tower. My eyes must have been bugging out with panic as I stretched my arms to work the valves to re-surface. I never thought about the scuba gear that was behind the seat. Had the RFS-1 not responded to my control inputs, I probably would have drowned.

This problem occurred because the water pressure inside of the conning tower increased with depth, as anticipated, but it also caused the rubber cover over the tower to expand outward, allowing water to come up higher on the inside. That was unexpected.

The condition was later corrected by placing two eyebolts, one on each side of the inside of the rubber cover, positioned just below the engine. A three-inch diameter hole was cut in the metal skin of the tower on each side to allow access to the eyebolts. After the cover was in place, the pilot would connect a cable with a turnbuckle to these eyebolts to draw the sides inward. Also, the shape of this rubberized, bulletproof bomber gas tank was conical and came to a blunted point at the top; this was where trapped air compressed. To reduce this air space, Don folded this cone forward and downward on top of the engine, tying it in place with rope to the wing roots. These changes prevented further expansion when diving deeper. (The same cover was used on both Mod 16 & 17).

The next boo-boo occurred because the main ballast valves did not have separate handles. One handle was used for all four valves. During one of the tests, I dropped the handle under water. As I grabbed the flashlight to start searching for it, the light went

(Fig. 6-9) Don watches closely as Bruce opens the valves to submerge.

(Fig. 6-10) The bow and starboard wing tip goes down nearly ten feet during first tests.

(Fig. 6-11) Tests for various attitude control.

(Fig. 6-12) Don watches closely from a submerged
out-crop of land during initial dive tests.

(Fig. 6-13) Perfect control with valves closed, wings level and decks awash.

(Fig. 6-14) Don struggles to couple the broken air line with electrical tape as water is being blown into his face.

(Fig. 6-15) Don is shown kicking his way clear near the stern after the hose repair. The RFS-1 is again at full surface.

(Fig. 6-16) The nose can clearly be seen bent upward after striking the bottom. Don is still in the water at the bow.

out. With panic hard to contain, I groped around in the darkness until I found it underneath my seat pan. Don later corrected that with a separate handle permanently mounted to each of the four valves. He also put window ports in the rubber cover to admit some daylight through the murky water. Two new flashlights were also stored inside.

The most terrifying diving experience occurred when the main external two-inch air supply hose broke apart during a test and the RFS-1 dove bow down, hitting the muddy bottom. My father was in water over his head at times, trying to reconnect the two pieces of hose together with plastic electrical tape, while air pressure was blowing water into his face (Figures 6-14 and 6-15). I was yelling into the sound-powered phones and getting no response. I never felt so alone and helpless. I had no idea what was going on, except that I might die!

After just a few minutes of what seemed like an eternity, the RFS-1 began to respond to valving air into the bow primary and secondary tanks to re-surface. I did not know that my father was in the water trying to repair the broken hose. Had I known, I probably would have freaked out.

After that particular test, Don removed the cover, and I gingerly stepped outside. The bow section was noticeably bent at an upward angle, but still intact and functional (Figure 6-16).

All in all, the RFS-1 Mod 16 worked quite well as a submarine. All of the "bugs" were worked out satisfactorily, and a few improvements were added in the new Mod 17. Now let's fly it!

Chapter 7. The Crash!

MY FATHER AND I HAD JUST COMPLETED some diving exercises with Mod 17 late on a busy Saturday afternoon in September 1962. Many small airplanes were taking off and landing, as usual. Don used his car to pull the RFS-1 out of the pond. It took some time to prepare it for flight, and the sun was at a low angle to the horizon. We needed to work fast if we were to fly it, because it soon would be dark. Together, we removed the tow line and all tie-down lines for the rubber cover, installed the propeller, reconnected and tested the air speed instrument system, and completed the preflight.

The engine was started, the control surfaces were cycled and tested satisfactorily; then it was onward to the taxiway. As I looked around for other aircraft, I could see that it was busy and waited until it was clear to proceed onto the active runway. The taxiways generally ran from the office building and hangar area, around both sides of the pond, intersecting the main runway nearer the middle than the ends. There was no separate parallel taxiway to the main runway. This meant that once you got to the main runway, it was necessary to expedite taxiing down to the take-off end of the runway so that no one would land on top of you.

Taxiing and maneuvering became interesting after a recent rain because of the many mud puddles and ruts. Many planes had become mired in the mud and ruts and had to be pushed out with people pushing on the wing struts. The taxiways were defined by the warn paths left by repeated traffic in the short grass, with no perimeter markings.

I took one last look at the windsock and tetrahedron. This is the large wind direction indicator, which somewhat takes on the shape of an airplane and is placed on a swivel pedestal located in an open area of the field. There was little wind from the northeast, so I selected the longest runway heading east, taxied down to the west end, and turned around, while looking out for other aircraft in the landing pattern. I had done this several times in the preceding weeks, building my confidence, as well as getting the feel of the RFS-1 as it "got light" and more controllable, just on the threshold of flight.

Seeing no other aircraft approaching, I lined up in the middle of the runway as usual, thought to myself, "Here we go. This is it. It's getting dark, so it's now or never!" I then applied full power. As I gathered speed, I watched the indicated air speed, which started at 40 miles per hour, continued past 45, then 50. I eased the stick further forward to raise the tail; it did not come up!

Accelerating through 55, then passing 60, the RFS-1 took off before I could abort, then suddenly climbed at such an increasingly steep angle that I could only see sky out of the windscreen. This rotation was so abrupt that I felt strong "G" forces pushing me downward into my seat. At the same time, my right hand was forcing the stick all the way forward instinctively. Then the door flew open, which caused me to look out of the left side, over my shoulder, to see the ground fading back and away. Knowing that something bad was happening, I felt sure that the elevator control rod either buckled or disengaged.

All of this happened in seconds, but I will never forget that it seemed a lot longer. I also remember talking to God. As the airspeed dropped to zero, the RFS-1 fell off to the left, with the nose pointing nearly straight down. I remember bringing the throttle all the way back, as I asked, "God, how am I ever going to get out of this?"

It was all like slow motion, as the earth came rushing back at my face. I pulled the stick back hard, all the way into my gut, and the nose started to come up. But it was too late. The RFS-1 slammed into the ground nearly flat, at about twenty miles per hour forward speed, and heading in exactly the opposite direction of takeoff. It had made a 180-degree turn in the air.

Dazed, I could hear a terrible racket and felt everything shaking. After a time, I began to focus on what was happening out in front of the windscreen. The propeller had ripped through the hull, and was still running! I also felt this numbness in my right foot. Everything seemed blurred. Then I finally managed to gather myself in and turn off the mag switch, cutting the engine.

Sensing that I had somehow survived, I peered out of the left port, where a Plexiglas window used to be, only to see my father with his wind-up 16-millimeter movie camera still in his hand, running over towards me. Even though it was becoming dusk, I could see that he was nearly white as a ghost.

I climbed out as Dad yelled, "Are you all right? Are you all right?" I replied "Yeah!" and told him what I had experienced, still checking myself for injuries. After a few minutes, my Dad asked why I had on a red sock and a white sock. The red of course was blood streaming from a gash in my shin from where a steel motor mount came down into my leg. My shoe caught my eye too, because I could see three or four bright shiny hash marks from where the leather toe area of my safety shoe was cut by the prop, exposing the steel toe guard. That explained the numbness I felt before. The big knuckle of my right hand was also bleeding from where the control stick slammed forward on impact, throwing my fist through the airspeed indicator glass on the instrument panel.

My father immediately took me to Fitkin Hospital to have the wounds tended to. They were not serious. On the way back to the airport, we talked about what could have gone wrong. Some witness said the RFS-1 went over 100 feet high; others said less. It felt like a mile to me!

After examining the wreckage, we discovered that water from the submarine tests earlier in the day had become trapped inside of the tail section, causing the center of gravity to be well aft of design limits. In other words, it was tail heavy; the elevator controls were not defective or broken. This was an engineering oversight; inadequate water drainage. To that, I say nobody is perfect.

Chapter 8. Change Strategy

THE DAY AFTER THE CRASH, several people at the airport helped load the wreckage of the RFS-1 onto a borrowed flatbed trailer for transport back home. After surveying the damage in his side yard, Don knew that Mod 17 was finished (Figures 8-1, 8-2 and 8-3). Had it not been for the out-of-balance condition, it was clear that the RFS-1 was capable of flying.

As I looked at the terribly deformed cockpit, where the fuel tank was only inches above my head and the engine's up-draft carburetor only inches in front of it, I thought to myself, "It just wasn't my time to go." The bottom of the hull was flattened, the landing gear had gone up into the wing roots, and the propeller tore a two-foot gash through the top of the hull and cut ballast lines in half. "So I bent it up a little; no biggie." I was a cocky 25-year-old with a cavalier attitude. I needed to be, or I would not have been doing that kind of dangerous activity. The double two-by-six wing main spar did not break, attesting to the strength of this home construction.

After a week or two of reflection, Don was back at it again, with renewed interest. He began to disassemble the wreckage and salvage what usable parts he could find. The new design became Mod 18 (Figure 8-4), featuring an all new aluminum skin conning tower, long rectangular windows for better visibility, a new instrument panel, a tricycle landing gear, hydraulic nose strut,

radio transceiver with dyna-motor, and storage batteries. It was
shaping up into a real beauty. He installed a McCaulley Clip Tip
aluminum propeller that was bigger in diameter, which
necessitated cutting out a section of the top of the hull and
fiberglassing it in to allow clearance for a bigger prop arc. Mod
18 was near completion by March 30, 1963, just about six months
after the crash.

*   *   *

Don was full of enthusiasm as he incorporated innovations
into this new model. But he overlooked one important thing. As
he went over the weights and balances, he became painfully aware
that the 65-horse power motor would not get this bird into the air.
It was too heavy (Figure 8-5). He couldn't afford a more powerful
engine, so he pondered for a while to rethink the whole thing.
Then he came up with a new strategy (Figure 8-6).

Don picked up a pair of Aeronca C-3 floats from Savannah,
Georgia, for $100, loaded them onto the roof rack of his 1963
Chevy II station wagon, and brought them home (Figure 8-7).
They were made of plywood, weighed 90 pounds each, and were
in great shape. Now he had a whole new plan. He reasoned that
since testing the RFS-1 could only be done on weekends, when the
airport was at its busiest, a floatplane could be tested in areas not
so busy. On water, the RFS-1 could go directly into the wind
without a crosswind component, and runway length was
practically unlimited for his purposes. Besides, the RFS-1 was a
boat and a submarine as well.

Inspired by his new concept, he removed the wheels, nose
strut, batteries and radio gear, and replaced the heavy "K" ship
pitot system with a simple, lightweight Piper design. Next, he
mounted the new floats to the inside of each main landing gear
mount, using steel tubing and aluminum reinforcing struts. Then
Don added a retractable water rudder to the back end of the port
float. After rebalancing it, the RFS-1 was a lot lighter and ready
to fly as Mod 18B in the river.

Incidentally, by 1963, the RFS-1 had a unique pedigree of
official documentation, starting with a New Jersey Certificate of
Ownership or Title, and Experimental Aircraft number N 174 D

(Fig. 8-1) This photo shows a smashed wing root and engine mounts that had shifted forward and downward, the prop had cut a slice in the top of the hull severing ballast lines and hitting the pilot's foot. The airspeed indicator was "punched" out of the instrument panel by the pilots fist, still tightly clasped around the control stick. A steel engine support member came down and hit the pilot's shin bone.

(Fig. 8-2) The remains of Mod 17 in Don's side yard, showing the splintered prop, deformed cockpit, cut air lines and gashed hull.

(Fig. 8-3) Damaged left wing root.

(Fig. 8-4) Don Reid stands on RFS-1 Mod 18 under construction, showing the nose wheel and metal prop.

(Fig. 8-5) Don contemplates the weight of the hydraulic nose wheel and strut, steel support frame with two storage batteries. The radio transceiver with its dyna-motor will be placed on top of the batteries.

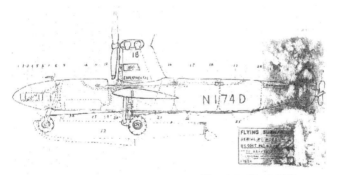

(Fig. 8-6) A new idea emerges. Floats! Mod 18B would solve many airport problems.

Aeronca C-3 floats from Savannah, Georgia.

Floats on the ground (in front of Mod 18).

(Fig. 8-7)

issued by the Federal Aviation Administration. It also had a boat registration, NJ 18 S, issued by the New Jersey Department of Conservation and Economic Development (as it was called then). Then there was the Marine Radio License, WZN 9048, issued by the Federal Communications Commission. And finally, the trailer tags TBJ 559, from the NJ Division of Motor Vehicles. As part of the ensemble, we included the chase boat with a registration of NJ 8433 N. In January of 1965, the Federal Aviation Administration issued a new registration number. It became N 174 R. Don interpreted the numbers in this manner: the 174 stood for the fourth test of Mod 17, while the D suffix in the original number stood for Donald, and the new R suffix stood for Reid.

Chapter 9. A Funny Thing Happened

DON SELECTED A SECLUDED BEACH CALLED Sands Point on the northern tip of the Port-au-Peck area of Ocean Port, NJ. The coordinates were approximately 40 degrees- 19 minutes-50 seconds north latitude, and 74 degrees-00 minutes-25 seconds west longitude using January 1945 Datum.

There happens to be another coincidence here, because we tested the RFS-1 on the same river where Mr. Simon P. Lake tested his original submarine invention of 1898. A model of Mr. Lake's invention is on public display at the Atlantic Highlands Municipal Yacht Basin and Park. Like me, Mr. Lake also lived in Toms River.

This sparsely populated shore of the Shrewsbury River was ideal to conduct further testing of the RFS-1 (Figure 9-1). That was a 14-mile round trip each time. Since the RFS-1 no longer had wheels to run on for towing, Don built a special transport trailer. It was simply made, with a long axle spanning to the outside of each float, connected to other pipes which formed an "A" frame, with the apex at the hitch. Large wooden planks were mounted on top of the framework with cross beams to support the two floats of Mod 18B.

It took an hour to transport the RFS-1 one way from home to the river, and of course an hour to return. The round trip travel, setting up, testing, and tear down during the short winter daylight hours was quite a task. There were times when we either forgot something, or had to carry extra cargo that required two trips. We sometimes tested until dark, even in the cold of winter, and always on a Saturday for many years. In the beginning, Dad tried different routes to find which was the least busy. He would even plot and make notations about the roads while pleasure riding in the area with his wife June.

*   *   *

A funny thing happened on West Park Avenue, in Ocean Township one day. On the way out to the test site, a trailer tire blew out with a bang in front of a residential house. As we were changing the tire, a police car came zooming toward us with lights flashing and siren screaming, skidding to a stop. The officer rushed over to us and asked rather excitedly, "Was anyone hurt?" We said "No. Why?" He said that a woman just reported a plane crash! After we explained to the officer what had happened, we all had a good laugh.

We usually had help assembling and disassembling the RFS-1 at the beach launch site. This would sometimes include my mother, my sister and her boyfriend Chuck, my oldest son Bruce Jr., friends, and even a neighbor (Figure 9-2).

During river testing, the beach area where we always launched from was very busy one day, with small sailboats milling about. I found it very challenging to maneuver a watercraft with a 28-four foot wing span in boat traffic! I delighted in the fact that other boats always yielded, regardless of who had the right-of-way. Sometimes we had a Marine Police escort to help out, but it was never a real problem.

One time, about two miles from the launch site, Mod 19E blew an oil line and had to be shut down. It was then towed back with our chase boat. We always had a chase boat for observation and photographic purposes, a 14-foot molded plywood run-about, with a 25-horsepower Evenrude outboard motor. A week later, the RFS-1 returned the favor by rescuing the chase boat, towing it back to shore from a mile away after its motor quit from dirt in the fuel. This was the first official SAR (search and rescue) mission for a flying submarine!

(Fig. 9-1) RFS-1 at the beach launch site in Port-au-Peck. This was the perfect place to test from.

(Fig. 9-2) Carol Reid and Chuck Lazarr help to assemble the RFS-1 at the launch site.

(Fig. 9-3) By nightfall, the damaged RFS-1 had been hauled back from the pounding surf to a spot on the beach close to the boardwalk, just south of the Asbury Park Convention Hall.

(Fig. 9-4) Two Asbury Park police officers inspect the RFS-1 papers, then check the rules book.

Another time, we launched the RFS-1 into the Atlantic Ocean on the Asbury Park side of the big Lock Arbour jetty in Asbury Park on February 14, 1965. We knew that there was an older, submerged jetty a few hundred feet south of the big jetty, because years earlier Dad used to fish from it, and I used to spear fish and scuba-dive near the end of it.

While taxiing straight out through the breaking waves between the two jetties, the RFS-1 did fine, but I was nervous. It was taking doses of sea water through the prop. I turned south toward the Convention Hall too early. I felt a thump, and knew that I had hit the submerged rocks; they came out further seaward from the beach than I had thought.

The starboard float was holed in compartments three and eight, and was taking on water. As I taxied off shore, I needed more power and left rudder to keep from turning right and crashing into the Convention Hall a couple of blocks away. (This was many years before the protective offshore rock sea-wall was placed in front of the building.) At this point, I was committed to follow through and use all the power and rudder I could, just to clear the last concrete pillar of the building, missing it by inches. To let up would have been disastrous.

I continued on, and ran the RFS-1 as far as I could right up onto the beach on the south side of the building, then anchored it into the beach sand to prevent it from sliding further back into the water. The tail was being severely damaged from the pounding surf, while Dad went back to the launch site to retrieve the long planks and tow-rope (Figure 9-3).

Then two of Asbury Park's finest blue coats (Figure 9-4) walked out onto the sand, stood by the RFS-1, asked to see our documents, and said "What happened?" We told them that we more-or-less "crash landed" here. "Mr. Reid," one said, "We'll have to cite you for unlawful parking of a vehicle in a public gathering area without a permit, City Ordinance number (whatever it was), of the Code Enforcement Regulation." Well, we needed this aggravation about as much as a submarine needs screen doors!

With pencil in hand, the officer looked at the space on the citation entitled "Vehicle Description," repeated it slowly aloud, looked at the RFS-1 again, chuckled and said, "It's not an airplane, a car, a submarine or a boat. What is it?" Dad looked straight in the eye of the cop and said with a serious look, "It's a flying submarine, sir!" The cop said, "Well, there's nothing like this on our books, and I'd rather not try to explain this to my superiors!" With that, he slapped the ticket book closed, turned and both of them walked away shaking their heads!

We dragged the RFS-1 across the sand, up close to the boardwalk next to the Convention Hall, and put it on display for the week-long, annual boat show. The plan had been to try to get airborne off the backside of a swell and demonstrate its capabilities, if all went well. So much for that plan.

Chapter 10. Variations, Concepts and Jet Engine

THERE WERE MANY DESIGN VARIATIONS and new concepts for each model of RFS-1. Most of the changes were instituted as a result of earlier design deficiencies or poor performance.

Mod 18B was the first to be tested at the new site on the Shrewsbury River, and that test showed that some major changes were still required. Although the route, system of transport, and the site picked for testing were all good choices, the first water tests told us to go back to the drawing board.

The two biggest problems were poor lateral stability and continued lack of visibility. The RFS-1 would tip from one side to the other very easily, causing the wing tips to make contact with the water (Figures 10-1 and 10-2). This was because the floats were placed too close together, inside of the landing gear mounts. The enclosed conning tower restricted flight visibility to the point where safety was compromised. The pilot could not see other boats on the water nearby or seaplanes in the air. There was, in fact, a low-flying seaplane in the air on at least one occasion.

To correct the visibility problem, Don made a radical change by moving the entire cockpit forward, out in the open, in front of the conning tower. It was actually a second, separate cockpit. The pilot now became the nose weight, and flight operations would be conducted from here. Submarine operations were still accomplished from within the conning tower, as before. The fact that the aircraft engine's propeller was only 18 inches behind my head did not bother me then. Thinking back though, I must have been out of my skull!

The floats were repositioned for the best estimated hydrodynamics and correct center of gravity by moving them to the outside of the landing gear mounts. This gave the RFS-1 a wider stance for better lateral stability. Incidentally, a third propeller was tried, another wood one with a different pitch, diameter and cord. The trailer also had to be modified to accommodate the new RFS-1. These and other changes resulted in Mod 19 (Figures 10-3 through 10-10).

*   *   *

Don bought a surplus Pulse Jet engine in the summer of 1964, in order to develop thrust augmentation, or JATO (Jet Assist Takeoff) capabilities. It was made by the Globe Company, Aircraft Division of the Solar Aircraft Company in Des Moines, Iowa. It was nearly seven feet long, with a 7-inch nozzle. The part number was 10P250, serial number 0645 of Globe Series S-42. This engine could produce 110 pounds of static thrust. It was originally made to power missiles and drones. This engine weighed about forty pounds and was made of monel. It was designed from the same type of engine that powered the infamous German V-1 Buzz Bomb or "Doodlebug." It was actually a larger version of the Dyna Jet and M.E.W. engines that we used on Mod 10 during our earlier model testing, and worked on exactly the same principals.

We tested the jet engine by itself at the Robert J. Miller Airport (now Ocean County Air Park) using a special mounting fixture for the engine. This was secured to Don's car with a heavy nylon line. We fueled this engine from a pressurized fuel cell. A lawn mower-engine-driven, high volume air blower provided the air start, and a six-volt Model "T" Ford spark coil fired the igniter on the engine.

While testing, the jet engine produced large orange balls of fire, and blasted blackened craters in the sand (Figure 10-11). That was exciting, and I could feel the concussions from the thunderous, explosive pulses. This engine was temporarily

(Fig. 10-1) Mod 18B tests showed limited cockpit visibility, and poor stability. The wing is shown touching the water.

(Fig. 10-2) This photo shows that the floats are too close together, making Mod 18B unstable, as Don restarts the engine.

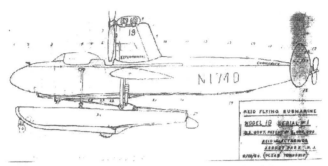

(Fig. 10-3) Rough drawing of Mod 19 which features floats mounted outside of the landing gear struts for better stability, and a forward cockpit for unlimited visibility for flight. The conning tower would still be used for underwater operations.

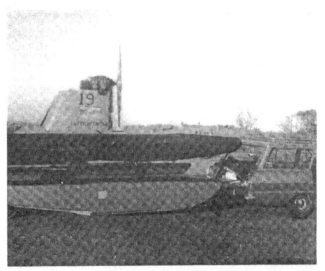

(Fig. 10-4) The new forward cockpit with the propeller only 18 inches behind the pilot's head!

(Fig. 10-5) On this day the crew was (L to R) a helping friend, inventor Don Reid and pilot Bruce Reid.

(Fig. 10-6) Getting ready to try out Mod 19.

(Fig. 10-7) Inventor Donald Reid is pleased with tests results of the RFS-1 Mod 19C.

(Fig. 10-8) Don Reid sits in the cockpit of his flying submarine invention.

(Fig. 10-9) Don Reid starts the engine of his flying submarine under trees in the side yard of his home.

(Fig. 10-10) Inventor Donald V. Reid sits in the cockpit of his flying submarine.

Working the controls.

Watching yellow flames.

Hooking up fuel lines, air hose and spark coil.

(Fig. 10-11) Views of pulse-jet engine being tested.

(Fig. 10-12) Don is in the cockpit of Mod 19C with the Globe pulse-jet engine mounted between the floats, under the hull.

installed between the floats of Mod 19C (Figures 10-12 and 10-13). Because of the lack of a special fuel control regulator that we could not get at that time, it would not sustain itself or keep running. So Don put the engine aside. I still have this pulse jet engine today.

*   *   *

More instrumentation was added as an aid to performance analysis. It included an eight-millimeter wind-up movie camera that was placed within a waterproof housing which I made, then mounted on top of the starboard float to show the position of the flight controls at any given moment. The aileron rods, rudder and elevator surfaces were marked in strategic places with brightly colored tape to indicate relative position for the camera. Several mechanical accelerometers were placed at strategic locations to indicate "G" forces for vertical, lateral, acceleration and yaw characteristics. They left tell-tail marks on special paper using a silver stylus on each. Even though homemade, they worked well and were calibrated on a certified centrifuge. Subsequent tests showed a marked improvement in performance with unlimited visibility.

On November 20, 1965, Mod 19C provided promising results in one test. With winds southeast at 18 knots, the RFS-1 reached 52 mph indicated airspeed . . . on the threshold of flight (Figures 10-14 through 10-18).

In May of 1966, the elevator was modified to enable the twin rudders of Mod 19D to be fully bi-directional by cutting a pie section from each end of the elevator, then changing the rudder horn arrangement (Figure 10-19). This enabled the rudders to become twice as effective because they now could both be deflected by the same amount and in the same direction.

Don went as far as he could go with Mod 19 and all of its derivations, and wanted to shed the one-hundred-eighty-pound pair of floats plus mounting hardware. During the summer of 1967, he designed and tested a radically new concept for a single float used with wing-tip pontoons to keep the RFS-1 wings level.

After a few rough drawings, he proceeded by making this single float with a few ridged structural members and aluminum sheathing. It was lightweight and had a large step in the bottom near the middle. The back of this step had large holes to allow water to freely enter and exit. The float was about two feet wide and twelve feet long, with two internal rows of thirty-gallon plastic tanks, four to each row, connected with air lines, along with relief and control valves.

Tests were conducted with this new float between the Deal Lake railroad trestle and the Main Street bridge in Asbury Park. Don would tow the float behind his chase boat at a relative high speed using a long towline. He weighted the float down by mounting external plastic tanks filled with water, on top. This simulated the weight of the RFS-1. He wanted to see if the float would lift the weight up onto the step and plane off like a boat moving at high speed. It did this very well after several tries. Don fitted this new single float about a foot below the center of the hull of the RFS-1.

Don then fashioned a pair of homemade, adjustable wing-tip pontoons, which were actually made from two halves of a Styrofoam-filled fiberglass shell. These shells were made by fiberglassing over molds that he made from pre-shaped, three-foot pieces of telephone pole. After the fiberglass cured, he cut the molds in half, then removed and discarded the wood, leaving the shells. He filled the shells with Styrofoam and glued the two halves together to make one pontoon. To finish the job, he inserted two, three-foot long aluminum tubes into the top of each pontoon, one in front and one in back, then pinned them into place. These tubes were then inserted up into each wing tip, and pinned. These and other changes made this RFS-1 into Mod 20 (Figures 10-20 through 10-22).

We tested Mod 20 with this new float concept several times on August 1, 1967. Although it sat well in the water and did get up on plane, it was too low to the water and created too much water splash and drag to get up enough speed to take off. After all of that work, this idea was tossed as well.

Mod 21 was born on September 2, 1967, with a single surfboard slung about eighteen inches below the center of the hull, using the same wingtip pontoons, only retracted all the way up under each wing (Figure 10-23). This idea reduced the weight even more, allowing the RFS-1 to float on the surface with its own

(Fig. 10-13) The air inlet of the pulse-jet engine can be seen just above the front tip of the float.

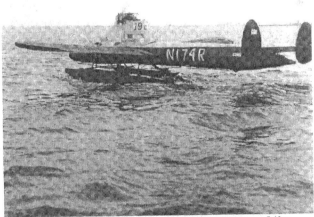

(Fig. 10-14) Taxiing out into the open water of the Shrewsbury River.

(Fig. 10-15) Taxiing out. Notice the white Chlorox bottle behind the engine. It is attached by a lanyard, and automatically deploys as a marker in case the sub breaks up and sinks to the bottom.

(Fig. 10-16) Wind SSE at 18 knots, Mod 19C best indicated airspeed of 52 mph.

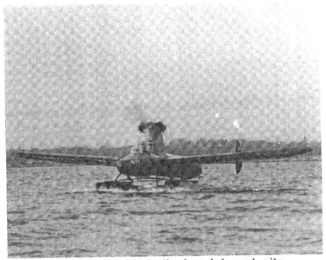

(Fig. 10-17) Returning to the beach launch site after a test run.

(Fig. 10-18) Shutting down after tests.

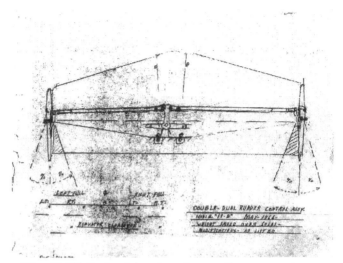

(Fig. 10-19) A pie-shaped wedge section was cut from each side of the elevator, enabling each rudder to deflect in both directions together.

(Fig. 10-20) Mod 20 with the single float concept and extended wing pontoons is being tested.

(Fig. 10-21) This shows Mod 20 with excessive wake turbulence and drag.

(Fig. 10-22) Testing Mod 20. Notice the wing pontoons are extended down on rods.

(Fig. 10-23) Mod 21 with a single surfboard concept and retractable wing pontoons being tested on the Shrewsbury River. Ballast tanks were added to each lower side to help raise the sub higher.

(Fig. 10-24) Mod 22, a pure jet-powered version in Don's side yard.

(Fig. 10-25) Various aspect views of the jet-powered Mod 22.

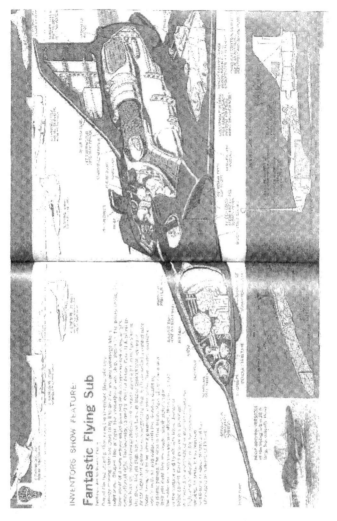

(Fig. 10-26) A viable concept on the centerflold of the <u>Popular Mechanics</u> magazine.

ballast system. The surfboard was supposed to lift the RFS-1 up out of the water like a hydro-ski, allowing it to plane off before flight. But tests showed otherwise. It looked good in the water, and would taxi nicely, but that was all. Too much drag, and too much water went through the prop wash. So much for that idea.

*   *   *

As a radical departure from the usual shape of the RFS-1, Don designed and built a full-size mockup of a delta wing, pure jet version of a flying submarine. He used such parts as a Navy F-4 Phantom fighter plane's back seat canopy section and his pulse jet engine mounted within. It was a pretty clean looking swept wing design, which he designated RFS-1 Mod 22 (Figures 10-24 and 10-25). It was completed in September of 1967. He had no intention of making it work, although it looked more like a modern aircraft with a future (if manufactured by a large corporation).

This was one viable concept that Don fervently hoped that the United States Government would fund and develop. A two-man version of it was featured in the centerfold of the September 1967 issue of Popular Mechanics, pp. 114 and 115 with story, photo and diagrams (Figure 10-26).

*   *   *

The next major change to reduce weight and drag was to remove the entire heavy landing gear mounting hardware. Two surf boards were then placed side by side like the floats were, and three plastic ballast tanks were encased within an aluminum shroud, complete with air lines and valves on top of each surfboard. The front and back ends were faired in to make them smooth and streamlined with suitable lightweight cones, and the whole assembly was mounted under each wing root using structural steel struts and tension rods. Then the struts were streamlined by riveting aluminum fairings around them. This, along with a different paint scheme of silver and gray, different fuel tank and other smaller changes made it into Mod 23, completed by fall of 1968 (Figure 10-27).

Tests showed that although ballast control of the floatation surfboards worked while standing still, the RFS-1 tended to nose over when power was applied because of the high thrust line and short floats. Similar performance results persisted for Mod 23B, C, D and E through November of 1968. Don made a few more changes, with a lot more fairing to streamline the surfboard pontoons, to become Mod 23F, and later G (Figures 10-28 through 10-30). What a difference in performance. Now it got up and went! It reached a speed of 60 miles per hour indicated air speed, felt light and controllable, just on the threshold of flight. But the RFS-1 needed more power! Given enough power, even a brick will fly!

Every weekend in November, Don tweaked and tested the final model of the RFS-1, Mod 23H, which could hop off of swells using ground effect (Figure 10-31), then settle back down; it could not sustain flight for any long distance, but it did fly!

(Fig. 10-27) Mod 23 had two short surfboard-floats and a high thrust line, which made it nose over easily when power was applied suddenly.

(Fig. 10-28) Inventor Don discusses the flight syllabus with pilot son Bruce in Mod 23G.

(Fig. 10-29) Getting ready to test with the help of a
neighbor and friend.

Taking the RFS-1 apart.

Tests completed, getting ready to go home.

(Fig. 10-30)

(Fig. 10-31) Now we're cook'in! Lift-off.

(Fig. 11-1) Don Reid looks over his abandoned RFS-1 project in the side yard of his Wanamassa home.

Chapter 11. The End of the Line

DURING EARLY DEVELOPMENT, the RFS-1 did not take off at all. Many, many ideas and concepts were tried for many years to perfect it. Many types of float concepts were tried, from a single hydro-ski, to multiple flotation surfboards, to a single self-draining, ballasted step float. It later became clear to Don that the 65-horse-power engine was not enough to sustain controlled flight. It required more power. Eighty-five horsepower maybe, but 110-horsepower would do it for sure. He did not have the money to continue or to buy a more powerful engine. So after Mod 23H, the project ended.

If nothing else, Donald Vernon Reid will go down in history proving that the idea of a flying submarine worked, in however limited a capacity; it did perform under water, very nicely I might add, and could be controlled while briefly in flight. If he could do all of this by himself, with his limited resources, just think of what a large corporation funded by the government could do, even with the state of the art as it existed then!

While the RFS-1 lay dormant in the side yard of his Wanamassa home (Figure 11-1), Dad retired from the Federal Government in 1971. For the next few years, my parents spent their winters in Florida. During this time they rented out their home with my wife, Bobbie, and me as agents. In 1974 they moved to West Palm Beach, Florida, to permanently be near his brothers and their families. He finally sold his home in 1979. But before he could sell his home, he needed a place to put the RFS-1, or else it was destined for scrap; a valuable piece of aviation history would be forever lost.

Don advertised in a small, local newspaper for a "home" for the RFS-1 as a historical item. He even spoke with the curator of the Smithsonian Institute in Washington, D.C., who said that they would like to have it, but did not have the room to store it just then, while they were finishing the new building (the present Air and Space Museum).

Some time later, a woman (who's name shall remain anonymous) from Tucson, Arizona, responded to Dad's newspaper ad. I do not know how she came across it. But Bobbie made arrangements to put the woman, her teen-age daughter, and her young son up for five days at our house, while the RFS-1 was being made ready for transport on a twin axle car carrier trailer. This woman had purchased the trailer from an acquaintance of mine in Toms River. These total strangers had 100% freedom of our 900-square-foot home while my wife and I worked during the day.

In October 1979, this woman trucked the RFS-1 cross-country to Tucson, where she was to place it in her new "AQUA" museum, one she did not have yet, nor did she ever get. My wife received a couple of phone calls from people across the country, asking for verification of this woman's story about the RFS-1. I well understood their curiosity, because this was one strange looking craft. The woman later called us to relate her cross country travel experience and told us that there was a reception parade, including the Mayor of Tucson, upon her arrival in Tucson with the RFS-1.

So Tucson is where it sat, in her driveway along with other assorted "stuff," for many, many years. We did not investigate her motives at the time because we were desperate and thankful that someone could use it. She talked a good story of her intent, but her dream never came to fruition.

Chapter 12. Displays, Lectures, Movies and TV Shows

WHILE STILL ENGAGED IN THE EVOLUTION of the RFS-1, my father was involved with many publicity events. He saw an opportunity to display his creation at the New Jersey Annual State Fair in Trenton, September 17 through 24, 1961. He was looking for support, recognition and money for the project. He set up a display at the south end of the race track grandstand, just outside of the main entry gates. He cordoned off the area with stakes, pipes and guy wires to hold up canvas and plywood walls. Then he made a blind entry with a table and chair for ticket sales, and charged 25 cents per person admission to see the "World's First Flying Submarine." The display area was adorned with placards and overhead strings of red, white and blue pennants. Behind all of this was of course, the RFS-1 Mod 16. He also set up a loud speaker system to use as a barker. Not to denigrate my father's efforts, but the display did look a little like a "Sanford and Son" project. Don stayed there overnight, sleeping in his car, parked across the highway after each nightly show closing. He took a week's vacation leave from his job.

I was very proud of him for accomplishing this huge task, mostly by himself, as I had a job to go to and a family to raise. I did, however, visit during the evenings when I could, along with my mother. He brought the RFS-1 to the fair, then back home to the shore alone, after a whole week of display!

Don did make a little money, but it was probably not worth the effort. He was gratified, and that was all that was important. That was the first of many public displays. As mentioned before, the RFS-1 was put on display at the Asbury Park Boat Show at the Convention Hall during the week of February 15, 1965, on the south side of the building, close to the Boardwalk.

He also displayed the RFS-1 at the Plymouth Meeting Mall in Bala-Cynwyd, Pennsylvania, during the last week of May of 1967. The mall paid for the transport of the RFS-1 to display it inside. Don mounted and hooked up a rotating red light on the top of the hull, as well as turning on the RFS-1 running lights. It was located in the middle of the mall in a roped off area. It was an impressive display, and the public ate it up.

I don't know what happened, except that after a few days of display, the mall managers and Don had a disagreement, and they refused to transport the RFS-1 back. He had a signed, one-way towing contract to bring it there, but no return contract. (Who knew?) So Dad and I disassembled the RFS-1 right then and there in front of the public, pulled it out of the mall, hooked it up to his station wagon at mid-day, and towed it home from Pennsylvania! It was slow going, with blown tires, traffic jams, burnt wheel bearings, darkness and other problems, but we finally got it home. I remember taking off work the next day to catch up on sleep.

On September 9, 1967, the RFS-1 was the main draw for the nine-day National Inventor's Exposition at the New York Coliseum as advertised in a feature article of the September, 1967 issue Popular Mechanics magazine. Although a great adventure for us, it, too, was plagued with problems.

The Expo movers loaded the RFS-1 onto a large flatbed trailer and trucked it to the shore area of Flushing Bay in New York, just off of the east end of a Laguardia Airport runway approach, to demonstrate it on the water before bringing it into the Coliseum. There was large white lettering painted on the black hull of the RFS-1 which advertised the "NY Coliseum."

First, my movie camera was stolen out of the back of Don's station wagon within moments of our arrival, as we were close by assembling the RFS-1. I did not mind the theft of the camera as much as the loss of the finished roll of film it contained. It was an irreplaceable film of a national TV show that featured my father and the RFS-1. Anyway, this particular model of the RFS-1 had the single hydro-ski surfboard, which meant that it would not take off. But we did manage to parade it around the Bay for a while.

Later, the Expo movers returned to load the RFS-1 back up and truck it over to the Coliseum, where Dad and I tried to set up the display. Mind you, all exhibits had to comply with a set-up format and be uniform. I said "tried," because almost every time we touched anything, some union member would yell at us. We quickly found out that each display set-up item was under a separate union. "You can't do that; only union contractors can!" "You can't plug in your extension cord; you have to call the union electrical contractors!" "Don't put up that curtain; only union building maintenance contractors can do that!" "Don't touch those rope stanchions; they belong to the union!" With all of the exhibitors setting up at the same time, you had to wait around to find a union person not busy. Being paid by the hour, they were in no hurry. Dad did not know how to play ball with the unions, and would not have done so if he did.

So we let them do everything, in their sweet time. Dad and I stayed at a local hotel every night to be nearby, at the Expo's expense (I think). On the last day of this Expo, Don had it up to his neck with their union regulations and opened up a display of his own. He became quite angry (like I said before, it takes a lot). After more than a week of being "controlled," he blew!

After having words with one union official, he looked at me with "that" grin again, and I thought "Uh - Oh!" Don quickly went over to the cockpit, pressing his lips tightly together, did something, reached up, grabbed the propeller and snapped it. The engine came roaring to life. As horrified people looked on, he went to the left side of the cockpit, and jammed the throttle full open! Wow! The sound was deafening, as I watched the large, blue backdrop curtains fly off in the wind and rope stanchions blow over, along with hundreds of all kinds of papers, brochures and flyers, both his and other exhibitors'; it did not matter to him. I grabbed the wing, trying to restrain the RFS-1 from sliding forward, as people scattered in all directions. After about ten seconds of what seemed like minutes, he shut it down.

Now they were really mad! Expo officials, security, and the

Fire Marshal came running over and told Dad to get that thing out of here, NOW!" Which was exactly what he wanted to hear. After his chewing out, bits of paper were still falling out of the air. I could not hold in my laughter. Transportation was guaranteed by contract. Even so, after all was said and done, the RFS-1 did suffer some minor damage. This was a prime example that Don did not always play by the rules, especially if provoked.

Everywhere we took the RFS-1, be it the airport, the river, or the ocean, it was always on display, even while stopped at traffic lights. People sometimes crowded around asking questions.

*   *   *

Don gave many lectures about the RFS-1, the first to the Delaware Valley Radio Association in October of 1957. The next was to the Experimental Aircraft Association, at the Bell Telephone Laboratories in Murry Hill, New Jersey, on January 6, 1965.

The State University College Science Club in Oswego, NY, provided the forum for his third lecture at Hillcrest Hall on May 12, 1966. The invitation included a pre-paid round trip airfare for Dad and me from Newark Airport to Syracuse Airport, NY, on a Mohawk Airlines Convair 404, a twin propeller aircraft, which landed in total fog. They also provided dinner for us. During this show-and-tell, they asked all of the right questions, and Don, of course, gave all the right answers. We were surprised to learn afterwards that our lecture followed the appearance of the beautiful Jane Mansfield the previous month. Those were big shoes to fill! The Club members were very cordial and hospitable, saying that they would welcome us back. Our return flight was on a jet DC-9, which was tossed around the sky in crummy weather. We had a lot of fun, even with the flight crew.

Don's fourth appearance was a 33-minute lecture with motion pictures for the Boy Scout's Father and Son Dinner, sponsored by the Methodist Church in Wayside, New Jersey, in the Youth Fellowship Hall, on March 14, 1969.

*   *   *

Around September of 1968, during the last stages of RFS-1 testing, Don received a telephone call via satellite from the Nippon Television Network in Tokyo, Japan. They wanted confirmation of the RFS-1 story, which Dad provided. They agreed to send a crew of three to make a documentary movie. Shortly thereafter, they arrived in Wanamassa and booked into a local motel for six weeks!

Mr. Harukiko Kawamura was the Program Director, Documentary Division of the Nippon Television Network Corporation. The sound technician and cameraman was Mr. Hideo Tsuchida, and the interpreter, Mr. Nagai Kuniaki. They used major amounts of film in the making of this documentary. They would first focus on Don and June's personal life by filming up close such things as Dad shaving in the morning, my mother cooking breakfast and stirring her coffee. They would "direct" by telling her, "Not that way; do it this way," while motioning with their hands. They recreated Don's travel to Washington D.C. by driving us around town, photographing downtown buildings, taking him to the bus station in Asbury Park, and filming him getting on a bus (something he would never do, because he would always drive himself). Back in Japan it would have more impact by doing it their way.

The Japanese crew was quite congenial, gracious and very professional, to say nothing of their enduring patience. They filmed the RFS-1 at the river test site (Figures 12-1 and 12-2). Unfortunately, the RFS-1 performance suffered during one submergence test, because a ballast tank exploded with a bang, causing the RFS-1 to nearly sink as it heeled over on its starboard side (Figures 12-3 and 12-4).

Holding a tall reed, pulled from the surrounding grasses, the producer held it high and moved it along in a big, slow arc as Dad, wearing his familiar baseball cap (Figure 12-5), followed it with his squinting eyes in the bright morning sunlight. He was being filmed by the cameraman who lay on his back in front of him, shooting up at an angle. It was to simulate Don watching his RFS-1 going through the air. They did several takes.

All three of the crew would accompany Don, filming him close up in the tiny chase boat, as he simulated "chasing" the RFS-1 during tests, waving his arms and shouting instructions. It was cold out there all day long in November, so the Japanese made a fire on the beach from the surrounding driftwood to keep warm. We all knelt around the fire to eat lunch and converse through the interpreter. I could feel the disappointment they must have felt by not seeing the RFS-1 go through the air during their visit. They filmed Mod 23D, E, F and G from October through November of 1968.

It was not until a week after they returned to Japan that Mod 23H gave the best performance of all. It quickly got up to speed, as fast as it would go, where it ran cleanly on top. Then I pulled it into the air for a brief flight, just off the surface, then it settled back. I did this many times that day.

Mr. Victor Beasely and his camera crew, from the United States Information Agency, Washington, D.C. visited Don to make a documentary movie for foreign release, this time to Africa. This only took one day to complete, and they did some filming of the RFS-1 at the same time the Japanese did. This was a 16-millimeter black and white film with sound. The personal interview was done in the evening in Don's home basement. He demonstrated how the idea came about, while pointing to things in his workshop. The final product was a short, well-edited documentary showing early historic flying machines and balloons, accompanied with music, leading into RFS-1 river testing, the interview, and ending with more historical footage with music. The film was called The Beasely Report.

*   *   *

Don was interviewed on radio talk shows on stations WFLN and WFIL Philadelphia, PA.

On December 24, 1965, Dad and I both were invited to be guests on the Amazing Randi Show that aired at 2:32 a.m. on radio station WOR Newark, NJ. That was a good, relaxing half-hour interview by a fun host, especially that early in the morning.

*   *   *

Don was invited to be interviewed on major television shows. The first was called Ten Around Town, broadcast on WCAU,

(Fig. 12-1) The Japanese film crew at the launch site.

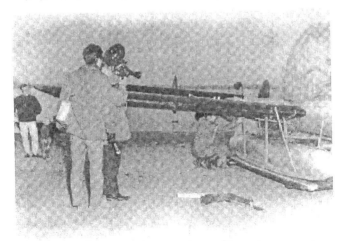

(Fig. 12-2) The Japanese film crew taking it all in.

Ballast tank explodes with a bank!

Safety lines are rigged.

The RFS-1 is towed back to the beach.

(Fig. 12-3)

Metal ballast tank shrouds have been deformed and displaced after the tank within exploded.

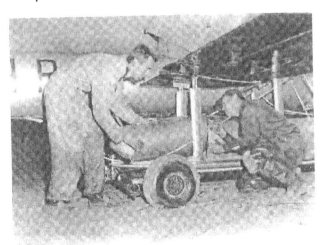

Don and Bruce examine the damage.

(Fig. 12-4)

(Fig. 12-5) Don, wearing his usual baseball cap, holds a line from the chase boat to the RFS-1.

Philadelphia, Pennsylvania. With these programs, he was given a good opportunity to tell his story to an audience in a wide area, even with limited airtime and selected questions.

On February 1, 1965, Dad and I both went on the CBS television show I've Got a Secret. They came to Don's house with a 40-foot enclosed van, loaded the RFS-1, and trucked it to the CBS Studios in New York City. We were there at the stage door when they started to unload the RFS-1.

As the RFS-1, Mod 19 was being rolled down the ramp of the van by the workers, Don walked into the van, grabbed the jet engine, put it on his shoulder and walked out with his valise in his other hand, fedora and dress top coat. One of the men yelled at Dad, "Stop! You can't take that; only we are allowed to carry that." Don just kept walking on into the building. I thought, "Here we go again!"

They set up the RFS-1 on the stage well before airtime, with the left wing bottom mounting pin removed, and a fine steel cable attached to the wing tip. With the wing pulled straight up, the stage curtain appeared as just a back-drop, with the RFS-1 secretly behind it.

The show's host, Steve Allen, came out, introduced himself, and reviewed with us what was to occur. I was six-foot-one-inch tall and had to look up at Mr. Allen. Boy, was he tall! Steve would relax before each show by practicing Yoga. He would stand on his head with his feet against the wall, balancing with his arms and hands in front of us, and an empty studio.

As time went on, the studio began to fill with people, and shortly before airtime, the panel entered and sat down. They were Bess Myerson, Henry Morgan, Bill Cullen, and Betsy Palmer. The televised intro and conclusion, along with the credits, featured songs being sung by Neil Sedaka.

During the opening scene, Steve Allen came out from behind the curtain at center stage and feigned a trip over something, then picked it up from the floor and sat down beside my father. Then Steve held up a large sponge, which said "Parking Ticket" on it. Then he squeezed water out of it onto the floor. He said he "just tripped over a parking ticket from a vehicle parked back stage."

The show revealed Don's secret to the audience. The secret was this: "My submarine is designed to fly." With that, the show proceeded with Bill Cullen narrowing down the secret. After the panel figured it out, the curtain opened, and the RFS-1 wing was lowered down into position such that Betsy Palmer reached out and touched it from her seat. While I sat in the cockpit wearing my crash helmet, I felt like a fish-out-of-water, and somewhat humiliated as I looked out over the crowd applauding and looking back at me and the RFS-1 on national television. I could sense the prying TV cameras in the very bright and hot stage lighting.

Henry Morgan asked, "What good is it?" The timing of that question was perfect for Don, as he unloaded the virtues of the RFS-1 while standing next to the wing and Steve Allen. It really went off nicely, and we had a good time. The Show paid Dad $80.00.

On January 14, 1966, Don became a guest on NBCs network TV show To Tell the Truth, hosted by Bud Collyer. This show opened showing our film footage of Mod 16 taxi tests and Mod 17 taking off into the air, followed by Don and the two impostors stating that they were "Donald Reid."

Bud Collyer then read the affidavit to the panel and the TV audience, stating who he was and what he did. It was now the job of the panel to figure out who the real Don Reid was.

The panel consisted of Tom Poston, Kitty Carlisle, Orson Bean and Peggy Cass. Time had elapsed, the panelists voted. Two of the four panelists got it right, and the host then asked, "Will the real Donald Reid please stand up." The program paid Don $20.00 for every incorrect vote, which meant that he had earned $40.00. But they gave Don the whole $80.00 anyway. He had a good time there, too.

Then Don had a 15-minute guest appearance on the Allen Burke Show, and on ABCs network TV show, The Johnny Carson Show. Although Don's story about the RFS-1 on this show could have been used as "cannon-fodder" for jokes, Mr. Carson respected my father's efforts and was sympathetic to his cause.

Throughout the 1980s, Dad appeared on local Palm Beach TV stations in what I call a desperate attempt to gain recognition and public support.

Chapter 13. Can the Military Use This?

IN THE MID 1950s, we had the bomb shelter craze. The situation was serious during the cold war with Russia. We had the distant early warning or DEW line in Northern Canada, and the Texas Towers off of our shores for aerial radar detection against the nuclear threat; that was it. Flying submarines, in the hands of an enemy power, could have entered the Hudson, Delaware and Potomac Rivers simultaneously, wiping out New York, Philadelphia and Washington D.C., while never having been seen on radar. All of this well before any retaliatory strike could have been launched. Don made the Pentagon people aware of all of this, and it seemingly fell on deaf ears.

*   *   *

On September 3, 1957, Don left descriptive material for review and consideration about the RFS-1 with Mr. L. M. Shields, Head of the Inventions Evaluations Branch, Office of Naval Research, Department of the Navy, Washington 25, D.C.. On the same day, Dad made an unscheduled stop at the northwest gate of the White House to deliver a signed statement to personnel from the Secretary's Office of the President of the United States. It was to inform President Eisenhower of his RFS-1 being the answer to this new and potential threat to our nation's defense.

The President apparently received the information, because in an April 18, 1965 article on page seven of the <u>New York Sunday News</u>, by Francis M. Stephenson, entitled "Inventor: 'I'll Get a Lawyer'";

Ike Voiced Idea

> While Reid was getting the horse laugh at the Pentagon, it so happened that the Commander-in-Chief, President Eisenhower, at that very time was predicting the invention of a flying sub. "Some day these will be able to fly across the ocean and submerge," we heard Eisenhower comment in September, 1957, as he sat aboard the atomic sub Sea Wolf off of Newport, R.I. He seemed to be thinking out loud. . .
>
> Maybe Ike told the military to get busy on a flying sub at that time. The Sea Wolf submerged that day in '57 and the ex-Army general seemed to have a lot of thoughts about it.

Don lectured about the RFS-1, using the jet-powered model, to the Delaware Valley Radio Association at the Mercer County Airport in October of 1957. After that, newspaper editors followed up on the story for years. He received a lot of local, national and international coverage through the Associated Press, United Press International and other press and magazine articles.

What useful purpose could the RFS-1 serve? Who needs it? "What good is it?" as Henry Morgan asked, on the network television show, <u>I've Got a Secret</u>. For Civilian applications, a one-or two-person private aircraft could fly out to a remote dive location or perhaps a resort island, land, submerge and explore a reef, wreck or whatever. For commercial, industrial or humanitarian efforts, the RFS-1 could be used for air/sea search and rescue, oceanographic research studies, under-water inspection of remote structures, or under-water environmental and ecological studies. The RFS-1 could also help out in law enforcement, especially in drug surveillance and interdiction.

Don tried desperately to capture the interest of the military, only to be laughed out of Washington. Don's first attempt was with a letter to the President dated March 6, 1955. Dad was then advised that the matter had been referred to L. S. Hardland, Assistant Chief Engineer at the office of the National Inventors Council. Dad drove down to that office on March 11, but there was no discussion because the letter had not yet reached the office.

I went to the Pentagon with Dad on some occasions during the late 1950s and early '60s, and we penetrated bureaucratic layers to talk to key personnel, one of whom was Eugene Handler, a hydrodynamicist for the Bureau of Naval Weapons. I do remember that the office of one individual we sought was insulated by no fewer than three layers of secretaries. Dad also met Captain W. F. Sallada from the Office of Naval Research in Washington to try to generate interest in his idea. Don wrote the Secretary of the Navy and received an answer back from the Bureau of Ships dated February 21, 1961. It stated that they would "be pleased to review any technical data," with the usual caveat of no obligation to the Government, signed by C. F. Elliott, Assistant to Chief of Bureau for Legislation and Special Matters. There were other visits too, but I do not recall the names, or dates of people we visited, and I did not go to Washington with Dad every time.

My father was asked by one of these high-ranking defense officials, whom I shall not name, "Fly a submarine? You must be crazy! Do you have any idea what one of those things weighs? You should be writing for the funny papers." We felt the sting of those hurtful remarks and deemed this tunnel vision on the part of our defense leaders. They lacked the imagination required to even consider the RFS-1. Many people visited or contacted showed interest and curiosity, but ultimately rejected the RFS-1 idea. We felt that they were either naive, or they were holding something back from us.

Later, Don found out that the government and a third party stole his idea and used his patented principles. He had data and documents to help support his allegations. Magazine articles began to appear from military circles to the effect that they were in fact looking for such a craft, a two-man craft capable of speeds to 150 mph, jet powered.

Mr. Roger P. Johnson, head of the Aero-Astronautics Department of the Rand Corporation in Santa Monica, California, paid a personal visit to Don's home early in 1965, and Don sold him a copy of his RFS-1 test results for $40.00. Mr. Johnson said, "We represent the U.S. Air Force, and our version of a flying submarine would make the Navy's look like a toy." Mr. Johnson said this to my father in front of me in the dining room of Dad's home.

The U.S. Government appropriated $45,000 for the analytical design study of such a craft. $30,000 of it was provided to Convair and Electric Boat Divisions of General Dynamics Corporation. The target completion date for their study was June of 1965. We felt that something was amiss, that something ominous was brewing. Don continued on by himself without government support, trying to promote the RFS-1 any way that he could.

The April 13, 1964, edition of Newsweek Magazine contained an article in part called "Search for the Flub (flying sub)," excerpts of which are quoted in context:

> "The Bureau of Naval Weapons is contemplating . . . an
> engineering study to perform analysis and preliminary
> design studies of the essential components and operational
> aspects of a full scale flying submersible vehicle . . . ."
> A flying submarine? At first glance, it looked like a wild
> idea but defense contractors who read this notice in the U.S.
> Department of Commerce's Business Daily (a bulletin
> giving firms notice of Federal government contract
> opportunities) a month ago have taken it seriously.
> By last week, dozens of large and small aircraft and
> shipbuilding firms (plus the usual scattering of cranks and
> backyard inventors) had written to the Bureau of Naval
> Weapons, and Eugene Handler, the Navy engineer
> responsible for the ad . . . .

I wonder how many of these "cranks and backyard inventors" held a U.S. Patent on a flying submarine and actually built one?

Of the many Pentagon people that we visited, Mr. Handler was the one Don spoke with at length, and with whom he entrusted his RFS-1 documents during the mid-to-late 50s. The article goes on to nearly duplicate the form, fit and function of Don's patented invention! The article continues:

> "The often proposed idea of a flying submarine isn't
> Buck Rogersish," insists Handler. For years, the 43 year old

hydrodynamics expert has been fascinated by the concept of a one-or-two-man craft which could fly at around 150 mph close to an enemy harbor or coastline, then land on water and submerge. Like a miniature sub it would continue silently - "at say 5 knots" - underwater for the rest of the way in, gathering intelligence or attack [sic] shipping, then turn around, emerge, and fly away. . . . "

Now where do you think he got that idea? Further on, under the topic of "Keeping Dry," Handler states:

". . . unfortunately, a plane is so light that to make it submerge even the cockpit might have to be flooded. We'd like to keep the crew as well as the engine dry," said Handler. "The pilot will have enough problems without adding the discomfort of sitting submerged in a frogman's suit."

Yeah, like me, the guy in his wet suit pictured standing on the wing of the RFS-1, Mod 16 at the Asbury Park Air Terminal prior to submerging. The article concludes:

". . . As a plane it will be inferior, and as a submarine even more inferior, but for the first time we will have something that can both fly and travel underwater. And that, for the Navy, would be very practical indeed."

In another article, which appeared in an Atlantic City newspaper dated Friday, November 27, 1964, in a column called More Than Talk, the headline reads, "U.S. Hopes To Get Flying Submarine," by William T. Peacock. It starts out declaring, "WASHINGTON (AP) - The Navy wants to develop a flying submarine." It goes on about war with Russia in the Black Sea and Caspian Sea, and recently let contracts that are mentioned in other articles. The point here is that it also refers to another publication in which Handler was quoted in the magazine U.S. Naval Institute Proceedings, a semiofficial publication. Handler states that "the development of a practical flying submarine prototype will be both complex and laborious, but the potential returns are substantial and valuable . . ."

The article continued with Handler's conclusion, but he upped the ante of parametric statistics a bit from a previous article, by referring to:

> . . . a possible craft with an operating depth 25 to 75 feet, submerged speeds 5 to 10 knots for 4 to 10 hours, airspeed of 150 to 225 knots for 2 or 3 hours, and payloads of 500 to 1500 pounds. He said it is believed these characteristics can be obtained within a vehicle weighing 12,000 to 15,000 pounds.

In other publications, there were many hilarious cartoons of flying submarines depicting them with periscopes sticking out of clouds and under water with fish and cruise ships, as well as perched on mountain tops; some showed political groups and armed service branches competing for potential flying submarine development dollars.   There were also jokes in print on the subject. Dad and I laughed at it all and felt that it helped our cause because it kept it in the public's eye.

There were many, many more articles written, but I feel the need to elaborate on at least one more, because it ties everything together and helps to reinforce my assertions.   Twin articles appeared on the centerfold of the Easter addition of the Newark Sunday News, April 18, 1965. The left-hand page shows a photo of Mod 19C, with the jet engine and my father and me, with an accompanying article by Francis M. Stephenson titled, "Inventor: 'I'll Get a Lawyer'." It starts out, "THE PENTAGON. . ." It was nicely written and tells our story. The right-hand page, however, shows the Navy's rendition of a flying submarine with a story written by Science Editor, Richard Lions. It is entitled, "Flying Sub, Ultimate Weapon, in the Works," and subtitled, "Navy designing attack craft - big Air Force concept looms as 'incredible'." The following are quotes from this article:

> Flying sub studies have been under way at the Bureau of Naval Weapons in Washington, the Air Force Development Planning Office at the Pentagon, the Electric Boat Co., Groton, Conn., Convair in SanDiego and the Rand Corp.,

Santa Monica, Calif.

A spokesman for Rand, the Air Force's West Coast "think factory," told a telephone caller who inquired about work on the flying sub:

"You called the right place - but we'd be dead if we talked about it."

'Creature' Designers Differ

An Air Force spokesman at the Pentagon confirmed that Rand recently finished a "feasibility and performance study analysis." He said the classified study was sent to Air Force headquarters by Rand, added that no action was pending on it now, then refused elaboration.

But details have been sifted from sources in Washington and at General Dynamics Corp., the huge defense contractor which controls both Convair and Electric Boat. These sources said two studies have been under way; [sic] one Navy, the other Air Force.

It was Convair that announced the concept of a flying submarine last month at a Navy anti-submarine warfare conference in San Francisco.

In an allied report to the San Diego meeting - which may have bearing on flying submarine development - Lockheed aircraft engineers announced the design of a jet propulsion system that swallows water instead of breathing air. They said this equivalent of an aircraft jet engine could drive ships at nearly 90 miles an hour, twice as fast as the swiftest surface vessel or submarine in service.

The Air Force concept is for "submersible aircraft" while the Navy's calls for a "flying submersible." The adjectival differences are important for they reflect the mission and attack mode of each design.

Combining the features of a midget submarine such as the U.S.S. X-1, and a fighter plane such as the Convair-designed F2Y Sea Dart, the Navy version would weigh about 8 tons and carry 2 men.

For Land or Sea

This version would take off from either land or water, fly to its target area, alight on the water, submerge for attacks on either surface ships or submarines, and then reverse the process for its dash home.

Such a version has been proposed by Eugene H. Handler of the Bureau of Naval Weapons, described as "the brains behind the flying submarine," and C. R. Tuttle of Convair.

Pentagon supporters of the Navy project seek to construct two smaller flying subs at a cost of "less than $20 million." They would be a blend of engines, air frame, electronic gear and weapons systems already designed and in use.

"This is existing machinery," said one naval engineer. "From an engineering standpoint the concept is neither as fantastic nor complicated as might be thought."

Other sources said, however, that the preliminary Air Force concept is much more sophisticated, even "incredible."

They said that the Rand "hydrocraft group" in Santa Monica, which is headed by Roger P. Johnson [the same person who purchased Don's test   results for $40], envisions a machine the size of a six-jet B-47 medium bomber capable of carrying nuclear weapons for a strategic attack role.

A Riot for the Imagination

The Air Force's submersible aircraft would be based under water where it would be least vulnerable to atomic attack.

My father and I deeply resented both Mr. Handler's pointed remarks, and the fact that he was being credited as "the brains behind the flying submarine." This was the U.S. Department of Defense official with whom my father entrusted all of his RFS-1 information. What a slap in the face!

*   *   *

The article continues, but the above gives a sense of what was happening in military circles. Throughout a 12-year period, beginning in 1957, Don received a lot of publicity about his RFS-1, most of which was very positive and helped his cause. However, the media blitz intensified, it seemed, after an article in the January 1, 1966, edition of the very popular, but now defunct Saturday Evening Post.

This was a beautifully written three-page story including the centerfold spread (pp. 52 - 54) entitled, "The Sub that Sails in the Sky," by Robert K. Massie. Pictured was a large broadside view of Mod-19 gaining speed on the water, along with two other photos.

From then on, many newspaper and magazine editors and columnists took up the story by calling on the phone to request an interview. It was like an explosion of journalism. It was amazing to me though, how many of them got the facts wrong (mostly newspapers) by misinterpretation, slant, bias or just plain distortion. Some articles even caused embarrassment for the entire family because of some untruthful assertions and misleading statements. It would be counter-productive for me to point fingers or specify the exaggerations. Suffice it to say that there were some outlandish statements published.

Other notable magazines included the May 1966 issue of QST, an amateur radio periodical (Dad and I were both ham radio operators W2FMG and WN2SMB, now N2LWF). Don used his ham rig on the water as "mobile marine," as well as the marine VHF radio WZN 9048. The article pictures him in his ham shack (p. 65); also shown is the RFS-1 during water tests.

The September 1967 issue of the Popular Mechanics (pp. 114 -115) features Don's RFS-1 along with an artist's conception of a modern, two-man flying submarine in a cut-away view, showing many unique accouterments on the magazine centerfold. Across the top are a sequence of drawings depicting a flying sub as it approaches to land on water, lands, submerges, resurfaces and takes off. That sequence also shows that the position of the water and air "doors" change position during the transition from flight to submerging, and vise-versa. The timing of this story was unique, because it announced the appearance of the RFS-1 as it was being featured in the nine-day Inventor's Show at the New York Coliseum.

The September 1967 issue of V*F*W* contained an article titled "Flying Under Water" (pp. 16, 32 – 33 at p. 33) by Walter B. Henderson, Jr., featuring the Navy's rendition of the flying sub, along with their story as well as ours.

The RFS-1 was pictured with a descriptive caption in the November 16, 1967 issue of FLIGHT International, under a column titled "Sports and Business" (p. 799).

Then there was a popular German periodical magazine called the Flug Revue, whose May 1969 issue featured our story titled "RFS Commander" (pp. 86, 88), along with three photos and text, all in German, of course. Generally speaking, this is primarily an air and space publication.

There was one other popular German magazine, Hobby, (Nr. 10/14.5. 1969) whose cover featured a beautiful and realistic artist's rendering of an action shot of a delta-wing flying submarine as it was approaching head-on and taking off from the surface of the water. The story was all in German, an eight-page spread (pp. 56 – 63) with photos of both the Convair XY2Y-1 Sea Dart and the Reid RFS-1, Mod 19. Both were action shots on the water.

In addition to the many newspaper articles published about the flying submarine, my father made mention of other major or familiar magazines which refer to it: "Flying Under Water," by Walter B. Henderson, Jr., Jacksonville Courier, Jacksonville, Ill., Aerospace News, April 26, 1965, p. 6; "Flying Submarine," Weekly Reader, October 18, 1967, Vol. 37, Issue 6, p. 2; "It's New," Mechanix Illustrated, February, 1968, p.72.

Don assembled a voluminous binder of newspaper and magazine articles about the RFS-1. I am sure that there was more written on the subject from many sources yet unseen.

Chapter 14. "The Missile the Russians Fear Most"

THEN CAME THE HEART-WRENCHING SHOCKER. In February 1977, a Reader's Digest article (pp. 129 – 132) by Ralph Kinney Bennett, broke the story of the "The Missile the Russians Fear Most." It was the Tomahawk Cruise Missile (Figure 14-1).

There are many versions of the Tomahawk cruise missile, such as air launched (from a bomber), ground launched, ship launched, and submarine launched. The submarine-launched version of the Tomahawk, which was designed to fit within the 21- inch torpedo tubes of submarines, was the particular version of great concern to us. When fired from the tube, its rocket motor propelled it through the water as it rotated upward, breaching the surface, continuing on through the air, while its propulsion systems transitioned from rocket to jet. While in the air, the tail unfolded and locked into place, as did the folded wings from slots within the body, and then the missile "cruised" on toward the target.

My father and I felt that this specific version of the Tomahawk was a direct patent infringement. It was clear to us from previous visits to Washington that the United States Government and General Dynamics Corporation stole Don's patented idea of an under-water-to-air vehicle. Our military used this unmanned version and programmed its guidance system, which later proved its value by targeting downtown Baghdad during the Persian Gulf War in 1991. On October 7, 2001, Tomahawk Cruise Missiles were again used against suspected terrorist targets in Afghanistan, after being launched from both American and British submarines. A newer version of the Tomahawk with greater accuracy was again launched from those submarines in the war on Iraq on March 20, 2003.

*   *   *

After reading the <u>Reader's Digest</u> article, Don chose to fight back; he gathered what evidence he could to prove his point, then (representing himself) filed suit against General Dynamics, who manufactured the Tomahawk Cruise Missile, as well as the U.S. Government, who funded and used them.

On June 12, 1978, he threw the first punch by filing a patent infringement suit against the United States Government in the U.S. District Court for the Southern District of Florida, in Fort Lauderdale. On July 27, the case was dismissed because the Court lacked jurisdiction over the matter. Don was directed to process it in the U.S. Court of Claims in Washington, D.C..

Don has been quoted in an article titled "Inventor fights for recognition of missile work" [sic] in a column called "Focus" in the September 21, 1989, Asbury Park Press, Ocean Edition, (p. B2), as having "approached more than 100 lawyers." He, mad as hell about it during the interview, may indeed have said that, though it probably stretched the actual number a bit. Even if it were only 60 lawyers, it was clear that most would not touch the case for any amount of money regardless of the outcome. Those that did express interest wanted a large sum of money up front.

In addition to Dad's attempts, Bobbie and I personally mailed out requests for legal assistance in this matter to no fewer than 44 select attorneys from around the country including Melvin Beli and F. Lee Bailey, who said "we can't help you." They cited caseloads, fairness to current clients, etc. Not one would take the case on a contingency basis. They wanted huge sums of money up front because of the time involved, size and complexity of this case. I still think that it was their loss because they had a good shot at a percentage of the multi-million-dollar military contracts.

After many failed attempts to obtain legal representation

The Missile the Russians Fear Most

Modern technology has transformed an old concept into an uncanny new weapon

By RALPH KINNEY BENNETT

It burst from beneath the sea in a white geyser, a slim 21-foot cylinder, small wings and fins snapped into position from its slender deck, shiny body as a turbojet engine roared to life and propelled it a thousand feet into the air. Banking, it angled downward until it was 50 feet above the surface, rushing toward land. Soon it was crossing over a green blur of trees, fields and housetops. To people on the ground it was noise and shadow, gone in an instant, a heartbeat.

A hill loomed before it. Inside the cylinder, a computer no bigger than a roll of bread pulsed a command through the guidance system; the missile tipped up slightly, cleared the hill and dropped down the other side.

(Fig. 14-1) The shocking <u>Reader's Digest</u> article of February 1977.

(Fig. 14-2) Don explains his dilemma to the media from his home in Florida.

during the next few years, Don did not quit. Instead, he became more determined to proceed with what he does best. He said, "If you can't go through them or over them, you go around them." He bought books, went to the public library and studied hard to learn briefing formats, different court requirements, and how to represent himself in various courts. Dad studied court rulebooks, learned how to prepare briefs, the number of copies and who to send them to, as well as the type and color of paper used. He said, "I have acted as my own attorney through all of this because nobody else would take my case." He was determined to tackle the "big boys" knowing that he would make mistakes. But he would do the very best that he could.

Litigation can become "wrapped around the axle," complicated, frustrating, convoluted and time consuming, to say nothing about the costs and strain it puts on loved ones. There are a lot of details omitted from this memoir, and there is no need to retry the case here, or be too specific. But in order to give a sense of the enormity of the task he faced, I've delineated the steps Don Reid took in his quest for justice by listing event milestones as best I can decipher them.

The sequence of events in the court battle went roughly as follows: in a second attempt at redress, Don filed his case in the U.S. Court of Claims in Washington, D.C.. It was docketed on October 6th, 1983, after an attempt a few weeks earlier had failed on rules and procedures. And on November 21, he added the third party defendant, General Dynamics.

On February 8, 1984, Don forwarded 57 interrogatories to both defendants to answer. By this time, the waters were starting to get muddy. Early in March, General Dynamics responded to Dad's interrogatories. Next, the Government requested more time to answer their interrogatories, a standard ploy in such cases. And in yet another document, the Government wanted to have the case dismissed, based on "old" stuff dating back to 1945, which Dad had included in his amended complaint. In mid-March, Dad received his ten books of evidence back from the Court; the court refused his new evidence. In April 1984, the Court ordered a hearing by telephone conference, which was set for May 10. On or about that same day, the Court officially denied Dad's offer of "new evidence." The next document that Dad received was the

Government's answer to some, but not all, of his interrogatories.

For nearly a year, litigation between the parties took on many aspects in the form of transcripts, briefs, amended claims, requests for time expansion, document exchanges, discovery, objections, a Contempt of Court charge, affidavits, responses, Court Orders, Decisions and Judgements.

I received a letter from Dad in April 1984, in which he stated that something "very big" was happening, and that he could not talk about it. He mentioned two new attorneys, and said not to talk to anybody about the RFS-1 unless they use the code word "ALLEN." I never found out what that was about, what happened or anything else about it. I subsequently forgot about it. I think one of the two lawyer's names was Davis from Washington, D.C.

Early in May 1984, Don provided answers to the Government's questions and objections to the Government's refusal to respond to ALL of his interrogatories. Don charged the Government with "Contempt of Court" for not answering his interrogatories. In late May, the Court ordered the Government to answer every one of Dad's interrogatories instead of only certain one. (Hey, he won one!)

In mid-September 1984, the Government filed a Motion for Dismissal, and provided operating details of both the Tomahawk and Harpoon cruise missiles. Also, the Government provided an Appendix – K, an affidavit in support of their Motion to Dismiss. Later in September, Dad responded to the Motion to Dismiss and the Appendix – K document with a rebuttal containing 41enclosures.

On December 18, 1984, at 10:00 AM, the teleconference "hearing" took place with the Honorable Judge H. Robert Mayer of the United States Court of Claims, in Washington, D.C. presiding, Attorney Jeffry H. Nelson representing the defendant, United States Department of Justice, in Washington, D.C., Attorney H. Cushman Dow representing the third party defendant General Dynamics Corporation, in San Diego, California, and . . . the plaintiff, Donald V. Reid, at his home in Florida, representing himself.

The day before this "hearing," I was in Mayport Naval Air Station, Florida, on unrelated business for the Department of Defense. As a result, it was by pure coincidence that I was visiting my father the next day when the call from Washington D.C. came in.

It was very hectic during the hearing because the small living room was full of books and documents, local TV camera crews, media interviewers, and family (Figure 14-2). Dad was trying to deal with all of this excitement during the hearing when he handed the telephone over to me after he realized that the Court was not going to allow any of his case evidence or expert witnesses. The Court later sent Dad a copy of the transcript of the telephone proceedings.

The Court had sided with the defendants. We were (I still am) confident that the case could have been turned around with more powerful counsel. No failings on my father's part; God knows he tried.   Unfortunately, the case was decided in a Summary Judgment, meaning that only the pleadings and the law were considered, not the evidence on the table. The case was decided on the technicalities of patent law, not evidence. In other words, the Court interpreted the law in accordance with the defendant's attorneys and the evidence was deemed irrelevant. Dad said that General Dynamics was arguing from the technical angle, while he could only argue from the historical angle since his diagrams could not be admitted as evidence.

On January 16, 1985, the Court ordered the defendant's motion for summary judgement be granted, and the case was dismissed without costs, meaning neither party could recover costs of suit from the other.

One week later, Don filed a Notice of Appeal and Brief on Appeal in the U.S. Court of Appeals for the Federal Circuit. On March 11, he received notice that he "had misdirected [his] your filing to the U.S. Court of Appeals for the Federal Circuit which is the appropriate appellate court but the notice of appeal must be filed here," (U.S. Claims Court).

Don straightened that out and received a Court docket number on March 19, 1985, along with a (needed) copy of their Rules of the Court, the <u>Procedural Handbook,</u> Entry of Appearance Forms, and Notices. As you can imagine with a case of this technical magnitude, there was a lot of legal maneuvering and transfer of paperwork between the parties.

In June 1985, Don provided a notice to the Appellate Court of temporary home address change from Florida to Arizona. On June 10, the Court of Appeals sent a notice to all three parties: "A review of this case indicates that oral argument is not required and that the appeal may be decided on the briefs . . ."   Also in June, the Court acknowledged receipt of Dad's six volumes of supplements.

On August 16, 1985, Dad's appeal was decided by a three-judge panel: "Non-infringement affirmed." Then the Court billed Don for costs of printing of his Briefs.

On August 29, 1985, Don again petitioned the Appeals Court, this time, for a rehearing in Banc. He was hoping to have a jury, charging violation of due process and theft of U.S. Patent by the Government. The same court denied the appeal on September 20, 1985, in a document signed by the clerk of the court and without specifying a reason.

Then on October 4, 1985, Don petitioned the Supreme Court of the United States for a Writ of Certiorari, challenging the decision of the U.S. Court of Appeals for the Federal Circuit. In order to obtain a Writ of Certiorari, a Constitutional issue must be raised. Don claimed (a) he never had the opportunity to show any evidence, (b) he was not allowed to present an expert witness, (c) the government used a patented device without compensation, (d) he was not allowed to have a jury trial, and (e) he claimed seditious libel and slander in tort (a reference to the fact that General Dynamics allegedly accused Don of obtaining his patent by fraud). Dad recited case numbers and statutes. Most important to his case was in a paragraph in Chapter 91 of the United States Code, which says in effect that inventors covered by patents, should be compensated for any invention that the U.S. manufactures or uses.

Don's petition was returned the first time on October 10, because he "failed to comply with the Rules." (Rule 21 and 46) He revised his petition with full Court compliance and resubmitted it with the proper format and use of rules on October 18th. On November 26, 1985, the petition was docketed in the Supreme Court of the United States. In mid-December, the Government Defendant waived its right to file a response to the petition in this case.

After eight years of frustration, Don got his case into the

highest court in the land. And he had done it alone! Not many people can get their case to this level without a lawyer on a singular issue (as opposed to a class action suit)!

If a Writ of Certiorari were to be granted, it would guarantee that the Supreme Court would at least review the case. If it were to find merit, the Court would call in the three parties for a full hearing. If not, the case would be dropped and Dad would have no further recourse.

Well, at least there was hope; Dad's foot was still in the door. Strangely, there was no more correspondence that I am aware of, until his request of the Supreme Court for counsel on August 27, 1986.

That hope died a week later when the last word came on September 5, 1986 in a final reply from the U.S. Supreme Court stating that Don's "Writ of Certiorari" was denied on January 27, 1986, and that "no further consideration of this case by this Court is possible."

Out of pure desperation, Dad pulled out all the stops and appealed for help from 22 Florida Congressmen, two Senators and President Reagan, citing discrimination against the elderly, among other things. He wrote the President on September 20, 1986 because it is the President who appoints the nine Supreme Court Justices, and documents from that Court must be signed in the name of the President of the United States. Dad later received a copy of the response from the U.S. Department of Justice – Criminal Division. They said, "No rights violated."

*   *   *

In retrospect, I feel that the Courts were wrong, and that they steam-rolled my father. He fought alone against batteries of lawyers who represented both defendants. I am proud of his efforts in spite of the outcome.

Just for the record, the cruise missile concept is an old one, going back to WW I. There were many types of Tomahawk cruise missiles that were not patent infringements, but the submarine-launched version is the one that Don Reid invented as the under-water to-air aircraft. Though different in size, construction and very minor aspects of technology, the basic under-water-to-air principles are the same: the vehicle is designed to be propelled and controlled under water, surface, become airborne, and perform a function through some type of guidance, in this case a one-way mission.

To reiterate, Dad's patent covered any means of propulsion, including multiple propulsion, electric, rocket, jet and nuclear; as well as any means of control, manned or unmanned; and any means of lift, including folding wings.

To further emphasize the point, the submarine-launched cruise missile, as we know it, is an airplane needing wings to fly. It is not a projectile and does not follow a ballistic trajectory. It is a controlled under-water-to-air flying machine, or submersible aircraft, whether it detonates on a target or returns from a mission for reuse.

Having just explored the legal steps taken in this case, I now want to touch on the sticking points. One of the major things the opposing lawyers pointed out was the fact that our RFS-1 had supplemental buoyancy in the wings, whereby the Tomahawk did not. We maintain that the supplemental buoyancy was selective, meaning that you did not have to employ it. It merely augmented buoyancy and control IF one chose to use it. The RFS-1 was so lightweight that it could be controlled under water by vectored thrust alone like the Government's Submarine Launched Cruise Missile (SLCM).

General Dynamics claimed that they used "gas" under pressure inside their SLCM to keep water out. In other words, it is pre-pressurized. We say so what? Their lawyers said that theoretically, adding more and more gas would make the SLCM even heavier, and therefore it would sink quicker. We say so what? What is the difference between "gas" and "selective supplemental buoyancy"?

All of these things that the flying submarine (RFS-1) has over the SLCM are improvement alternatives and enhancements over all other flying submarine patents. Key words in the Reid patent Claim 1 are "selectively rendered operative" and "means for rendering the supplemental buoyancy means inoperative." We say those changes and modifications falling within the scope of the invention by those skilled in the art are still part of the patent coverage.

As a final basis for their judgement, the Court cited case law, referencing a previous Court decision which said, in effect, that EVERY component in Claim 1 of the patent must be present in the accused device or else there is NO patent infringement. They said since both the General Dynamics Tomahawk and Harpoon SLCM do not have operating buoyancy ballasting in the hull or wings, there is no patent infringement. General Dynamics admits that "gas" does in fact bleed out from the pressurized SLCM as it is propelled to the surface of the water so that the pressure differential would not damage the SLCM during its assent. To me, that is venting, and a pretty fine line of distinction between theirs and ours. I'm not sure that doesn't go beyond splitting hairs.

Further, the Court stated that claims sounding in tort are outside the jurisdiction of the Claims Court, and that there is no right to a jury trial against the United States in the Claims Court.

In my opinion, the courts realized that Don was not an attorney at law, and that the courts did afford leniency and gave him every opportunity to go by the rules of the courts. They even provided guidance on procedures and deadlines. They "closed an eye" to his procedural errors in order to bring about a conclusion. They gave him his day in court . . . so to speak.

*   *   *

For a while in 1984, letters from Dad were coming to me at the rate of one per week, sometimes two. Most of Dad's letters were typewritten, some had hand-written notes in the margin. After many case setbacks by January 1985, Dad wrote in terms that he very rarely used, "The Government is screwing the hell out of me, and I'm getting awfully sore [about it all]." In spite of the outcome, I am very proud of my father for standing up to the corporate giants and the Federal Government for what he believed in.

This allegedly (I use the word allegedly for my own protection) stolen idea had a profound effect on world politics, economics, and freedom, and yes, it made a lot of people rich (and still does). This is the American way. But Don Reid has never been recognized for his efforts. He is just one more name on the list of American inventors initially overlooked for their achievements: names like Robert Goddard for rocketry and Simon P. Lake for his submarine. I was told that the Wright Brothers went to England to get their first patent on the airplane.

I quote the <u>Palm Beach Post</u> staff writer John Koopman in his December 13, 1985 article, "Juno Beach Man Fighting to Top Over Invention," p.1:

> Hollywood someday may make a movie about Donald Reid's fight to prove he invented the [Flying submarine/]Cruise Missile.
>
> It would be all about one man with 200 law books up against the combined might of the U.S. Government, General Dynamics Corp. and their armies of attorneys.
>
> And the battle would be fought in the highest court in the land, with Reid acting as his own attorney. . .

That would be really neat, and it would be prophetic if Mr. Koopman's idea came to pass. It is my wish that Don Reid's achievements be recognized somehow, someday!

Chapter 15. The RFS-1 Lives On

IN DEFERENCE TO MY MOTHER'S WISHES, by the mid-1970s (before the Tomahawk Missile revelations) my parents had moved to one of the rented homes of Don's brother Burtt on Dillone Lane in Juno, Florida (the street was named for Burtt's wife Dillone). Don didn't have the big basement workshop or spacious back yard that he once had at his Wanamassa home. He now had to be more controlled and get used to living with more rules, working out of a tiny shed in the back of the house. Although he never mentioned any of this to me, I knew my father, and he must have felt restrained, subdued and confined.

Don did a little fishing, rebuilt several broken and discarded outboard motors, and worked on motorboats to keep busy through the early 1980s. He even worked at a local marina, repairing boat engines or Travelifts (for carrying boats) to make extra money to continue his case. He was also active in the American Red Cross and ham radio.

Dad even found time to "create" another offshore racing powerboat from yet another burned-out 28-foot boat hull and five Scott outboard motors. He raced the boat here in New Jersey. But this downsizing changed his lifestyle and left him with fewer options to deal with the ever-present thoughts of the RFS-1 lawsuit after 1978.

Dad built a full-size mock-up of a cruise missile using the Globe jet engine that he had, and other special parts that he found, made or had made (Figure 15-1). He found an old broken boat trailer that he fixed up and converted to a "trans-launcher" for his cruise missile. This trailer was used both to transport the missile and to enable it to be elevated upward at an angle to the sky for firing position. After he had it all painted up with a silver body, white wings and tail, and a red nose cone, it looked pretty real, with its U.S. star insignia on the wing and body.

Because of the Tomahawk, Don now strongly emphasized the words "cruise missile" when referring to his new mock-up. He used it in an attempt to gain recognition and public support in his fight against the U.S. Government and General Dynamics Corporation for his belief that they stole his invention.

Dad, working alone, put his cruise missile on display at several shopping malls in the West Palm Beach area, along with placards, photos, news releases and patents. He gave many locally televised interviews from his home on the subject.

In 1986 Don's beloved wife June died suddenly from lung cancer. Six weeks later, his daughter Dorothy expectedly died from a brain tumor. He kept active, stayed "loose" by doing things that appealed to him in Florida. He did not want to go into a shell, and tried to fight off depression and loneliness by visiting my wife and me in Toms River, and my sister Carol and her husband Chuck Lazarr in Phoenix, Arizona, three and four times a year. He wanted his independence, no cages, and we understood that.

Although my father outwardly showed optimism, I'm sure he was frustrated and felt the futility that he was up against, knowing that time was running out. I could begin to sense the desperation of this man in his mid-70s. Lack of success with his lawsuit and the loss of loved ones may have prodded him to make a big stir to gain satisfaction and attention. Although he felt that he had nothing to lose at this point, we never discussed any motives for the following event.

Don arrived at our house from Florida with the cruise missile on the trans-launcher in tow. He entered our house, threw down a traffic citation on the table, and said with a broad smile, "Look at what I got! I'm keepin' this as a souvenir!" Bobbie looked at it

(Fig. 15-1) Don Reid's flying submarine [cruise missile] on a trans-launcher.

(Fig. 15-2) The RFS-1 Mod 23H is just rotting away in Tucson, Arizona.

(Fig. 15-3) The RFS-1 is being prepared to be towed back to the Lazarr's in Phoenix from Tucson, Arizona for possible restoration and display. Don is pictured at middle right.

and said, "Oh no you're not! You are going to pay it!" (Dad always liked Bobbie, and of course he paid the ticket.)

The ticket was a $35 trespassing citation that he received from the Washington D.C. police, after they finally decided how to deal with the situation. Dad recounted the story to us. On his way up to New Jersey, he decided to stop off in Washington D.C. on the afternoon of June 6, 1987, and park next to the fence in front of the White House with the elevated cruise missile facing the Capitol!

You can imagine the commotion that ensued. Capitol Security, Secret Service and the D.C. police came at Dad from all directions, with guns drawn! The Canine Unit and Bomb Squad arrived while Pennsylvania Avenue was being blocked off. Don was promptly arrested. He tried to explain that it was only a mock-up and that it was inert. As he started to walk over toward it, saying, "Look! I'll show you," he was grabbed, cuffed, and placed in a squad car. The investigating officials looked everything over, then simply cited Dad and let him continue on to New Jersey.

I truly believe that he was just trying to get photographs of his cruise missile with the White House in the background to use on the jacket cover of a real gutsy book he had written entitled <u>Secret or Top Secret</u>. Another reason I believe this is that I later found eight-millimeter movies of his cruise missile in front of the White House, before the Supreme Court building and in other areas in Washington. Don had already made several copies of the book, which had cut-and-paste facsimiles of the Capitol building, White House and Supreme Court on the cover. The gist of that book had little to do with the RFS-1, but with other experiences in his life.

*   *   *

Meanwhile, the RFS-1 sat for nearly 10 years in Tucson just rotting away under the blazing sun (Figure 15-2). Don thought about that stagnant situation and decided to do something about it. About mid summer of 1989, while visiting Carol and Chuck in Phoenix, Dad and Chuck planned to go to Tucson and bring the RFS-1 back to Phoenix to restore it. At Don's request, the woman released the RFS-1 back to him.

Chuck told me the story:

> We got all ready to start out and made it to the end of the alley, when the hitch on the trailer fell apart. After about an hour of jury rigging, we set out on the road again. As we were driving on the freeway back to Phoenix, I was wondering why everyone that passed us was pointing at the FS [flying sub]. I pulled off the road and we checked the trailer and the FS, only to find out that the darned FS had worked its way back until it was a quarter of the way off the trailer (more jury rigging to get it back on the trailer). Pop was really good at that sort of thing. All the traffic on the road was slowing down and everyone was waving and cheering us on as we finished our trip home.
>
> We had a great time, and it is something that I won't forget.

Dad worked on the RFS-1 with each visit, from two to four weeks at a time, bringing more tools from Florida and material from Toms River to make the RFS-1 as complete as possible for historical purposes. Perhaps it could be displayed some day (Figure 15-3).

*   *   *

It was around Christmas 1990 that Bobbie and I were traveling with another couple for an overnight stay in the Reading, Pennsylvania area to visit the outlet stores, see the spectacular Christmas lights, and enjoy the majesty of the countryside. On the second day, we visited the Reading Regional Airport where I had a chance meeting with Mr. Russell A. Strine, President of the Mid Atlantic Air Museum (MAAM). It was located within an old aircraft hangar at that time.

The site of the museum is on what was known as the Carl A. Spaatz Field, or Reading Army Airfield where bombers were housed during World War II. After the war, the buildings were used to show captured German and Japanese aircraft as well as experimental aircraft.

Founded in 1980, the MAAM's collection has expanded to

(Fig. 15-4) The RFS-1 is being prepared for transport to the Mid Atlantic Air Museum in Reading, Pa., to be restored and put on display for all to see.

AIRCRAFT
of the

MID ATLANTIC AIR MUSEUM

(Fig. 15-5)

January of 1937. During World War II, like many other designs already in production that were pressed into service, the aircraft filled many roles as a trainer and transport.

In 1954 Beech rolled out the Super with the "E" model, featuring a higher cabin roof, longer wingspan, improved engine cowlings, a larger door with a built-in air stair, and higher gross weight.

The Museum's G-18S Super

The G-18, introduced in 1959, added optional 3-bladed Hartzell propellers, a two piece windshield, a picture window in the cabin and other interior refinements. The gross weight was again increased.

The Museum's G-18S Super was originally owned by the P.H. Gladfelter Paper Company, of York, Pennsylvania. In 1962 it took top honors for its owner at the Reading National Business Air show, and was even pictured on the cover of 'Flying' magazine.

It was donated to the Museum in 1962 by a private individual.

CURRENT STATUS: Operational condition, on display.

SPECIFICATIONS
Engine: Two Pratt and Whitney R-985 (450 HP)
Wing Span: 49 Feet, 8 Inches
Length: 35 Feet, 2 ½ Inches
Height: 10 Feet, 5 Inches
Maximum Speed: 225 MPH

REID RFS-1
"FLYING SUBMARINE"
1962

Although the concept of a "flying submarine" provokes a reaction of disbelief in most people, it became the very real goal of inventor Donald Reid, after the idea came to him one day in his Asbury Park, New Jersey, workshop. His intention was to design a craft which could submerge, evade enemy radar, then surface and take off from the water to attack the unsuspecting foe.

Reid claimed success in the mid-1950's, when the RFS-1 reportedly submerged, surfaces, and then flew as an airplane. He received a patent on the concept in 1963.

Appearances before the Navy Department and the Military Invention Board proved both fruitless and frustrating... the idea was characterized as impractical and of no military value.

Reid achieved some attention with the RFS in periodicals and on such popular television shows as "I've Got a Secret" and the "Tonight Show". He later tried to develop interest in the flying sub as a sport vehicle, for underwater photography, salvage, and even air-sea rescue. He continued to develop and refine the design and modified the RFS-1 some sixteen times over the next several years.

The RFS-1 ready to take off during tests conducted in the 1950's

In 1977 Reid became aware of the Navy's Cruise Missile Program, which included a submarine launching of a submersible guided missile which Reid felt infringed upon his patent. Despite his

- 33 -

(Fig. 15-6)

efforts to receive proper credit for the concept he was defeated in court.

The Reid Flying Submarine was donated to the Museum in 1990.

CURRENT STATUS: Unrestored, in storage.

> **SPECIFICATIONS**
> **Engine:** Lycoming 0-145 (65 HP)
> **Wing Span:** 34 Feet
> **Length:** 26 Feet
> **Height:** 7 Feet
> **Maximum Speed:** 87 KTS
> **Maximum Speed:** (Submerged) 4 KTS

SIKORSKY HH-52A "SEAGUARD" 1962

On May 14th, 1958, the Sikorsky Corporation test flew its first amphibious helicopter, the S-62. The S-62 incorporated much of the earlier design features of the S-55 and S-58 models, but was designed with a watertight fuselage and two outrigger floats, which also housed the retractable landing gear. The S-62 was also the first turbine powered helicopter to be certified for commercial use.

In 1963 the United States Coast Guard received the first of 99 HH-52A aircraft - a search and rescue version of the Sikorsky S-62.

The Museum's HH-52A, 1394, was stationed for a time at the Coast Guard station on Cape Cod, and was last assigned to the Coast Guard at Chicago, it is preserved in those markings. It was acquired through a trade with the US Naval Air Museum at Pensacola, FL.

The HH-52A carried up to twelve passengers, and was produced in both military and commercial versions.

CURRENT STATUS: Operational, on display.

> **SPECIFICATIONS**
> **Engine:** General Electric T58-GE-8B (660 SHP)
> **Rotor Diameter:** 53 Feet
> **Length:** 44 Feet, 6 ½ Inches
> **Crew:** Two
> **Range:** 474 Miles
> **Maximum Speed:** 109 MPH

CONVAIR CV-580 "ALLISON PROP-JET" 1962

Searching for a reliable, economical, high-speed short-haul aircraft to replace the DC-3 after WW II, major airlines turned to Convair. Seating up to 52 passengers, the Convair model 240 became the first modern post-war airliner.

The Convair 240 first flew in March of 1947. One hundred were already in service by 1948. Plagued by structural design problems, the Convair liner's main competition, the Martin 2-0-2 and 4-0-4 never overcame the head-start or popularity of the 240 and later models.

With the onset of the jet age, the Convair design proved its versatility. The improved models, Convair 340's and 440's were adapted for turboprop powerplants, improving their efficiency and extending their useful life.

34

nearly 75 restored and unrestored aircraft ranging in age from the late 1920s to the mid-80s. Their mission is to preserve aviation history, and to educate our youth. It is a "flying museum," meaning that many of their restored aircraft fly to other areas of the country to perform or be displayed at air shows. They put on their own great World War II Weekend air show annually.

Mr. Strine showed us around and explained in some detail the many interesting aircraft and artifacts. He pointed out the 1964 Custer "Channel Wing." Of the three aircraft that were built, only two still exist: MAAM's and the one in the Smithsonian National Air and Space Museum. I mention this aircraft because of the very distinctive "U" shape to each wing within which was placed a pusher engine. The propeller arc nearly touches the "U" shaped wing surface.

One other aircraft that Russ showed us requires special mention here because he took some time to explain with pride. It was in twisted, bent-up pieces of aluminum with some parts in wooden box shipping crates. It was a complete Northrop twin engine P-61B "Black Widow" night-fighter which had been equipped with radar. There are only four of these aircraft known to exist, and its remains were retrieved from a mountain crash-site called Mt. Cyclops near Hollandia Airfield in the Pacific. It took extraordinary effort, diplomacy and money by Russ and his father, Gene (Pappy) Strine, to recover this relic. As I understood it, this crash site was a sacred place to the local natives, as was the aircraft itself. To remove the aircraft and other missing parts later found, MAAM was required to pay money, barter and trade items to satisfy their gods and local officials. One of the items traded was said to be a newly restored PT-17 bi-plane.

This very rare P-61 aircraft became the catalyst for the museum. This particular P-61B will be the only one in the world to be restored to flying condition! Great progress has been made in its restoration to date by many dedicated volunteers. It is a thing of beauty.

Mr. Strine stared silently with unbelieving eyes when I told him about the RFS-1, and explained that if he wanted to own this strange asset to restore and add to his unique aircraft collection, it was his for the taking as soon as I cleared it with my father. Russ, an accomplished pilot and aviation historian in his own right, expressed his desire to add the RFS-1 to the museum, and cheerfully accepted the offer. It would be a fitting addition to the unique and rare offerings of MAAM.

During a telephone conversation with my father in Phoenix, I told him what we would like to do with the RFS-1 (bringing it back to the MAAM), and his last words to me were, "Go for it son, . . . go for it." Two days later, my father died of a brain tumor in Carol and Chuck's home on the morning of February 6, 1991. He was 79.

We did go for it. I called MAAM and told Russ of my Dad's passing; now with a sense of urgency, I requested them to pick up the RFS-1. It took some coaxing because the idea apparently met with some degree of skepticism and perhaps even opposition by his advisors or staff members. Ultimately, they had a planned trip to deliver an aircraft by trailer to a place in California, then decided to stop by the Lazarr's in Phoenix to pick up the RFS-1 and truck it back to MAAM (Figure 15-4).

The first thing that the museum did was to remove the engine for proper storage until their new building was completed early in 1993. Although restoration of the RFS-1 is planned, there have been delays in the museum expansions and other issues. As of this writing, the completion of the RFS-1 restoration is anticipated soon.

The museum published a 41-page aircraft guide entitled Aircraft of the Mid Atlantic Air Museum (Figure 15-5) by Pete Malashevitz, with graphics and documents by Hank Bowman. The RFS-1 is on pages 33 and 34, and is one of the many aircraft listed in the guide. This guide shows a photo of the aircraft along with a brief history, statistics and current status (Figures 15-6 and 15-7).

When the RFS-1 is restored, I have requested the Museum to dedicate a memorial plaque to honor Donald Vernon Reid for his contribution to the field of aviation and to recognize him as an aviation pioneer. Unfortunately, many pioneers are not recognized in their own day, but posthumous recognition is, I suppose, better than none.

About the Author

Bruce D. Reid is the son of the inventor and actively participated with his father in the design, construction and testing of the RFS-1. He was born and has lived his entire life in the central New Jersey shore area.

His working life began mainly as an Electronics Technician, then later a Logistics Management Specialist in support of Naval and Marine Corps aircraft weapons systems at Navy Lakehurst, New Jersey. He has recently retired, and holds a United States patent.

Among his recreational interests are flying, boating, scuba diving, fishing, ham radio, model airplanes, travel and his antique car.

He has two sons from a previous marriage, and three stepdaughters from his present marriage. He and his wife now live in Toms River, New Jersey, and enjoy their winters in the Florida Keys.

Made in the USA
San Bernardino, CA
17 September 2017